Crossing The Finish Line

Dr. L.D. Holmes
William "Bill" Norris

Copyright © 2025 Dr. L.D. Holmes

All rights reserved.

ISBN: 979-8-9881137-3-7

Jarretts Publishing Company LLC

A HEAVENLY PERSPECTIVE

The owner of the tenement which I have occupied for many years has given notice that he will furnish but little or nothing for more repairs. I am advised to be ready to move.

At first this was not a very welcome notice. The surroundings here are in many respects very pleasant, and were it not for the evidence of decay, I should consider the house good enough. But even a light wind causes it to tremble and totter, and all the braces are not sufficient to make it secure. So, I am getting ready to move.

It is strange how quickly one's interest is transferred to the perspective home. I have been consulting maps of the new country and reading descriptions of its inhabitants. One who visited it has returned, and from him I learn that it is beautiful beyond description; language breaks down in attempting to tell of what he heard while there. He says that, in order to make an investment there, he has suffered the loss of all things that he owned here, and even rejoices in what others would call making a sacrifice. Another, whose love to me has been proven by the greatest possible test, is now there. He has sent me several clusters of the most delicious fruits. After tasting them, all food here seems insipid.

Two or three times I have been down by the border of the river that forms the boundary and have wished myself among the company of those who were singing praises to the King on the other side. Many of my friends have moved there. Before leaving they spoke of my coming later. I have seen the smile on their faces as they passed out of sight. Often, I am asked to make some new investments here, but my answer in every case is, "I am getting ready to move."

Author unknown

DEDICATION

I want to dedicate my part of this work to the memory of Sharon, my beloved wife, who has already made her heavenly transition, and to my three sons, David, Jason and Jon, who have and continue to make their father so proud.

CONTENTS

	Introduction	viii
	Preface	x
1	THE BEGINNING	Pg 1
2	PAIN COMES FOR A PERMANENT VISIT	Pg 8
3	THE CANCER JOURNEY BEGINS	Pg 23
4	A CANDID LOOK AT THE PROCESS	Pg 34
5	BE HONEST WITH YOURSELF	Pg 43
6	A WONDERFUL RESOURCE - - HOSPICE	Pg 49
7	DON'T STOP LIVING WHILE YOU'RE LIVING	Pg 56
8	A UNIQUE PERSPECTIVE	Pg 63
9	BILL'S TEACHINGS ABOUT HEAVEN	Pg 69
10	HOW THOSE WHO CARE, CARE	Pg 104
11	THE LAST CHAPTER	Pg 109

ACKNOWLEDGMENTS

Behind every good book are some great people who do the really hard work of bringing it into print. Thank you to Proofreaders, Kay Coward, and Cleo Feltner. Thank you for your attention to detail and on-point suggestions.
Special thanks to Ryan Martin, one busy man, who was never too busy to edit and format.

INTRODUCTION

I want to tell you a story. Not just any story, but a story about living and—dying.

Where to begin is the problem. There are really a lot of places, so I guess I will just begin in the middle and work from there.

First, a little about myself. I am a Pastor. I have worn the mantle for the past fifty years. It has been my unique opportunity to share some of the most important and happy occasions in a myriad of lives. Weddings, births, baptisms, family gatherings and similar life happenings have been a very real part of my life.

I have also walked the other side as well. Death, divorce, funerals, job losses, miscarriages, family trauma, and heartaches too numerous and intimate to count.

Indeed, it is one of those intimate experiences of life which forms the background for the story I want to share with you. I am not fully aware of where this story will take us. My prayer is at the end, you will have insight into one of life's greatest mysteries, and with that perspective, perhaps a different view of what lies in front of you.

At the expense of sounding to "Pollyanna" this is a story about living a good life and dying a victorious death. It is a story of the reality we all share.

Living...and... dying.

In this story you will meet my friend Bill. He has stage 4 prostate cancer. It will eventually take his life. You will walk with him through his journey of diagnosis, disbelief, and even at times discouragement. You will also share in his moments of new self-awareness and acceptance of his ultimate end. You will witness how a person of faith, while daily battling pain, sometimes excruciating and intense pain, finds a relationship with Jesus Christ he never thought possible. You will hear in his own words how this new relationship provides him an ultimate peace and security only experience can describe.

To be clear, this is not about a "salvation experience." Bill has loved and served The Lord for decades. This is a story about something much more intimate and rewarding! Something only a person who has accepted their own mortality, and looking forward to the next chapter can adequately explain.

Crossing The Finish Line

PREFACE

It was a good day! Spring was springing, birds were singing, green grass was appearing where ice and snow had prevailed for far too long, and the sun was finally shining again.

Then Bill walked into my office. Before we go any further, allow me to explain a few things about my friend. He is a student of The Word and has taught extensively on the Holy Scriptures for over 40 years. He quite possibly has amassed more Biblical study materials than some publishing houses. Whenever he taught a class, you knew instantly this was not just a class to listen in on, but rather an experience in discovery.

A few years before this Monday morning, Bill had received his diagnosis of inoperable stage 4 prostate cancer. At the time, he was teaching the largest Sunday School class in our Church. We are a large Church, and he had the largest room in the building, save the Sanctuary and Family Life Center. Rarely, if ever, was there an empty chair in his designated room. He continued to teach until he just literally could no longer continue because of the cancer's progression.

Now, back to Monday morning. After accepting a cup of coffee and answering a few questions about family, friends and life in general, he made the following statement: "Pastor, you know I have dedicated my life to teaching The Word of God, but because of this cancer thing, I just can't do what I have done in the past. I still want to serve. How can I be of service to The Lord and the Church"?

I have spent my life answering people's questions and looking for answers to a myriad of difficult situations. I am seldom without some kind of answer or option for them to look at or an opportunity for them to pursue. That was, until this Monday morning! I had absolutely no idea what to say or how to react to his question. I asked for a few days to explore some possibilities.

What do you say to an eighty-year-old, cancer ridden, pain wracked individual who wants to serve God? This was a man I respected who had served with distinction. That he still wanted to serve and give of himself says so much about his character and Christlikeness, but I was at a complete loss as how to respond.

As has happened so many times in the past, the answer came in the least likely of scenarios. It was in a Church staff meeting where I believe the Holy Spirit whispered the answer to Bill's question. I called Bill and scheduled an appointment to meet him at his home. I wish I could explain how I so did not want to tell Bill what I felt I needed to share. In fact, I was truly prepared for him to possibly become angry and ask me to leave. But, he had asked, and I believed the Holy Spirit had given an answer, so I felt compelled to respond. "Bill, you have spent your entire life teaching us how to live, what would you think about taking the last months of your life and teach us how to die"? To my great relief, Bill smiled broadly and said, "Let's do it".

We agreed to meet every Thursday Afternoon at 1:00 p/m. The plan was for me to ask a few leading questions about his week, and he would simply talk to me about it.

Months have now morphed into years, and we are still meeting, and I am still learning. I have never left one of our sessions in which I have not felt like I have been in the presence of The Divine.

Bill has talked intimately, openly and honestly about his journey. What a privilege it has been to walk with him through these days. You, dear reader, are now invited into an adventure few have ever experienced. In the process, you will hear some hard questions asked. You will, in return, hear some honest answers which, I believe, will perhaps change your whole perception about this thing we call death. After all, you are hearing it from a man who will have walked through the valley, and is waiting to experience a new morning on the other side.

Although he has never said, I believe Bill wants to share with you his daily experiences and inter-actions with his Friend and Savior, Jesus Christ. He has said repeatedly," without the abiding presence of God The Father, and His Son Jesus Christ, as well as the moment by moment influence of The Holy Spirit, life would be unbearable!" I think this will become much clearer as you experience his daily discoveries of what lies in his immediate future and how God is drawing him into a closer understanding of his spiritual destiny.

Crossing The Finish Line

1 THE BEGINNING

First, some background about Bill's early life as he tells it.

"I am follower of the Lord Jesus Christ. There is nothing special about me. Maybe that is why helping to write this book has been so enjoyable. As you read it, please consider the scriptures used throughout the publication. I have done my very best not to cause or create any blatant errors. If I make a statement not based on the scriptures, just take a moment to think about it, then move on to the next thought. I guess you could call this a story about an 81-year-old man who has experienced many unpleasant events but has found great help and solace in his relationship with Jesus Christ. I am not sure how long I have had this terminal cancer, but suffice to say, it probably started long before my initial diagnosis. A critical point I want to make here in the beginning, there has never been even one day that the Lord Jesus Christ has not been walking beside me throughout this journey. If you have not accepted Him as your Savior, much of what you read will not always make sense to you. (I invite you to think about allowing Jesus Christ into your life as Savior and Lord. It will make this journey of cancer look and feel so much different.)

I was raised Catholic and went to a Catholic grade school. I really did not have any say in my school choice, it was just what we did.

I remember it was a freezing Iowa winter, and I was an altar boy getting ready for the Christmas midnight mass. We lined up outside the church in the skimpy red cassocks and special white surpluses while waiting for the priest to start the procession. The wind was blowing, and snow was falling. The nuns were doing their best to keep the walks clear, while many of the guys were complaining and grumbling. Some were even using crude language, thinking the service would never start. All except one that I know of-me! God was warm and close in a way I had never experienced before. I did not tell anyone about this, as I would rather not be publicly embarrassed.

I must admit, I hated school. It was small, and we had to serve mass one week each month. The Monsignors were not always in a good mood, and at times even smelled of nicotine and alcohol. For whatever reason, I never seemed to experience the love of Jesus through the nuns or the clergy. Perhaps this was because of my age or personal perspective. I just knew I was missing something.

Because the school was small and only went through the eighth grade, I escaped to public high school. Looking back, I did not enjoy those four years any more than the eight years I had spent in the Catholic elementary school.

After high school, I worked as a waiter in a resort hotel in Asheville, North Carolina. At the time, I was not following a spiritual path, so will avoid most of those stories.

My father had an addiction problem that found me spending much of my time away from the house. The Cornhusker Tavern and back-room pool hall became my hangout. There was an older man there who would buy beer for those of us who were underage. I remember the cost was 25% plus retail. A case of twenty-four cans would net you eighteen. I was well accepted because I had a job and the cash to buy the booze.

Wig Wam grocery store was my first encounter with immorality. One of the store owners attempted to grab and fondle me in a very inappropriate way. I remember I said to him, 'get your hands off me, you queer S-O-B. A few days later, I was dismissed. I eventually got a job delivering papers for the local newspaper. I would note, God was not relevant or active in my life at this time.

Eventually, I got a job at the Western Electric assembly plant. I was also attending pre-pharmacy classes. I have often said if I had to make a living with my hands, we would be on welfare.

One day, I saw a recruiting advertisement for the Air Force. It caught my attention, and soon found myself in basic training. I would go to church on Sundays to get out of marching and 'housekeeping'. After basic training, I was assigned to an Air Force base in Amarillo, Texas. My job was to learn how to make reports, write about Air Force history, and eventually to work in Public Relations for the Air Force. Upon completion of my assignment my number one goal was getting out of that frozen base. My next assignment found me moving to Topeka, Ks., where I was stationed at Forbes Field.

It was during this time I felt God tugging at my heart. I went to the base Chaplain and told him I was afraid of losing my faith. I cannot remember his exact response, but it was something like, "Call somebody who cares". That really turned me off to religion.

While stationed at Forbes Field, I decided to get my college degree. It was in one of my college classes that I met this really good-looking blonde girl. After a time, her mother encouraged her to invite me to Sunday dinner. It definitely beat the chow hall, so I found myself at their dinner table every Sunday.

That blonde-haired beauty's mother Ruth prayed for me for three years to have a personal relationship with Jesus Christ. It was during this period that Sharon and I got married. She was a strong Christian and was not timid about sharing her faith walk with me.

Many of you will remember the great Billy Graham Crusades which crisscrossed our nation and world in the sixties. It was during one of those crusades in Kansas City (MO) that I accepted Jesus Christ as my personal savior. It forever changed my life's desires and direction."

UPDATE JANUARY 1ST 2022

This is my journey. It will be different for others. These are my thoughts based on my feelings and experiences to date. It is my prayer that it might help you to know your thoughts and feelings are felt by others and that you are not alone.

I often found my emotions would look like an EKG or a Sine Wave. It was times like this when I would pray, and to the best of my memory Jesus never ignored my calls for help. As the first five years came and went, I did fairly well handling both my wife Sharon's health issues and my battle with cancer.

The cancer at times felt like it was in a state of limbo. It really is hard to describe. To be fair, I do not ever remember feeling good physically, just less bad (I hope that makes sense).

Cancer, for me, has and seems to continue to be a fairly slow progressing disease, at least for the most part. One of the things I notice the most is how my fatigue level has become more oppressive.

I have had multiple surgeries for various things. As the increasing levels of pain became more intense, I was assigned a palliative pain team. The team consists of an MD, PRN-c and a Social Worker. I think this was around my 6th year from diagnosis. (I have the date but am just too tired to go look for it.)

The chemicals now being used to control pain are Fentanyl, Oxycodone, Hydrocodone, Gabapentin, and some OTC's. When I remember to take these on time it keeps the pain levels between 4-6.

We rapidly increased the ascending levels of cancer drugs, but they did not help much. This was when the doctor ordered six intervals of low radiation.

In one of my many trips to the Kansas City Medical Center, I was asked to participate in a National Cancer Institute study using the chemical "Olapradid" twice daily. To be honest, I really did not want to do the study, but then I figured somebody had participated in some of the drugs I was currently using, so I should pay it forward for someone else.

The disease began to accelerate, and I was once again referred to another highly acclaimed cancer center.

Then Sharon died, and my world fell apart. After 56 years of marriage, I experienced a loss so profound I still have difficulty coming to grips with it. I feel her presence with me daily. Family and friends have been so kind and attentive, of which I am so profoundly grateful, but I still miss my Sharon.

I had been a Sunday School teacher for decades. As the years came and went, I found myself becoming progressively weaker. Eventually I had to resign from my teaching position. It was just so painful to sit or stand for any length of time. I might add, this was one of the most difficult decisions I have ever had to make. I used to call teaching my "hobby horse," but in reality, it was learning and growing my relationship with God and then sharing what I had learned with others.

Every day I say I have cancer. To the best of my ability, I have owned it from day one. At the same time, I remind myself that Jesus is with me! I have done this almost every day now for over 2,600 days! In one sense, I suppose you could say it is simply a confirmation of reality. I do have a terminal disease that will end my journey here on earth. The good news is, I also know I have an eternity of perfect health ahead of me.

I have been asked a number of times if I am afraid of this cancer killing me. Here is where I stand in that regard. First, the Father has said when my work is done here on earth, He will take me home. Then, as I mentioned earlier, I have my "daily starter." I acknowledge and say, "I have stage four cancer," and I know it will eventually take my life. God, in His infinite mercy, has allowed me to see a glimpse of what "going home" means. He is also a gentle and loving teacher. He is teaching me new things daily about myself, my cancer, other people, and most importantly, about Him!

My Father knows everything I am going through, and I know He loves and cares for me deeply. I also believe He wants me to continue to learn some important Biblical truths.

One of those truths He has revealed to me is that He is more interested in having a personal relationship than He is about performances. Having repeated this truth for every day now for almost eight years, I become more convinced with each passing day. In addition, I have learned new and important truths about heaven, and how to communicate more effectively with the Trinity. I know I am just scratching the surface of the wonderful treasures He has waiting for me.

Crossing The Finish Line

2 PAIN COMES FOR A PERMANENT VISIT

"And in the same way the Spirit also helps our weakness; for we do not know how to pray as we should, but the Spirit Himself also intercedes with groanings too deep for words; and He who searches the hearts knows what the mind of the Spirit is because He intercedes for the saints according to the will of God. And we know that God causes all things to work together for good to those who love God, to those who are called according to His purpose."

Romans 8:26-28 (NASB)

Pain, is built into our DNA. In its simplest form, pain is the result of man's original sin. There is pain in childbirth, as well as pain in death. One of the unique things about pain is once it has had its way with us, its power is often diminished and at times disappears entirely. This is one of God's wonderful gifts. We remember the "event" but seldom the pain of the event. That is not to say we will forget there was pain, but rather we have physically moved away from it.

"To the woman He said, I will multiply your pain in childbirth, In pain you shall bring forth children." (Genesis 3:16 NASB). Most women would say the pain of childbirth is swallowed up in the exhilaration of the new birth God has given.

Jesus Christ, God's Son, The Second Person of the Trinity, suffered horrible pain before going home to The Father. Think about it, He was whipped with Cat-o-Nine tails, a crown of thorns thrust upon His head, hands and feet nailed to a Roman cross, and yes, even mocked by the very ones He had come to redeem. Pain, excruciating pain, both physical and emotional, assailed Him before death released Him into victory. I cannot recall anywhere in the Calvary event where Jesus mentioned His pain. Questions, yes! ("My God, why has Thou forsaken Me?") The pain was secondary to the event and resulting purchase of eternal life to those who believe.

In Isaiah 43 we find these words of assurance:

"Do not fear, for I have redeemed you; I have called you by name; you are Mine! When you pass through the waters, I will be with you; and through the rivers, they will not overflow you. When you walk through the fire, you will not be scorched, nor will the flame burn you. For I am your God, the Holy One of Israel, your savior." (Isaiah 43: 1-2 NASB).

Yet, seemingly beyond reason, pain has an undeniable way of getting our attention and re-focusing our thoughts. It even has an insidious way of making everything else in life seem secondary.

For those walking with one who daily experiences chronic pain, it is often difficult to see the invisible damage pain is causing. Because chronic pain is incredibly complex, it makes the one experiencing it even more so. A mild-mannered person may become irritable, impatient, and short-tempered. The naturally impatient and irritable person may become even more so. This is quite possible because pain just sits there, taking up space in the suffering of one's life. Frustration mounts and is typically displayed through anger and irritability.

I want to read you an e-mail I received from Bill.

(I do not believe in coincidences.)

"Here is a brief update on how not to handle cancer pain, or perhaps it is the way. Physical pain to be certain can be difficult, but I am more convinced emotional pain can be completely debilitating. On July 14th of 2023 I had my first Pluvicto infusion. It is an end-of-life drug used to keep the patient as comfortable as possible before moving from Palliative care to Hospice care. It is the strongest and a last resort cancer drug. I was emotionally in pain and tears because Sharon would not be there to go through it with me. The side effects were a high level of fatigue, difficulty concentrating, etc. Then two weeks later I had my quarterly chemo infusions at St. Francis. Those side effects are always bad, though mostly physical pain presenting itself. So, chemo on Friday and by Saturday I am a real mess. The physical pain was there, but even worse, my lifetime treasure was not. By Sunday, physical and emotional stress was even worse. I was wishing I had just started Hospice and got this over with. Then late Sunday evening, I had an "aha" moment. Bill, you dummy, you know and have taught that Jesus will be with you in your deepest need. You just have to ask Him. I did, and it was not long before I was back to normal. The lesson here, I think, is the worse it gets, the more you require Jesus. Reach out to Him, and If you are fortunate enough to have a good friend, call them.

You will have moments like these. They really suck, but when Jesus reminds you, He is there with and for you, it can become a teaching moment."

Before this, Bill had shared that he "believed suffering brings an intimacy with God that verges on a sacred fellowship that is difficult to put into words." For the one who is dealing with intense chronic pain and does not have Jesus to turn to and lean on, it can be all the more debilitating.

A fair question for both the one who is suffering, and the one walking with them might be: If God really does love us, and wants the best for us, why does he allow pain and suffering?

Before we attempt to walk into this thicket of thrones, we should understand, it is difficult, at best, to give a sufficient spiritual answer to an intellectual question. The spiritual and the intellectual exist in two entirely different universes. This should be emphasized over and over. The unbeliever, or the one who has neglected their spiritual person, will never be satisfied with a spiritual answer. Yet, if one is to ask a spiritual question, it seems we should pursue a spiritual answer and not one based on the intellect. The difference is the mystery existing between the spiritual (God) and man (experience) The spiritual quester seeks God and walks with a faith perspective. The intellectual quester seeks self-affirmation and walks with an experience perspective.

Physical suffering will on most days, remain a mystery. As you will see and have noticed in Bill's words, there are always lessons to be learned. Of course, when pain is intense and mind numbing, the last thing you are looking for is a life lesson, but learn you will.

With that in mind, let's examine what Bill, who has a deep and abiding relationship with Jesus Christ, has to say about physical pain and suffering. We will then look at someone who goes through this journey without that personal relationship to lean upon.

Bill states:

"It is difficult to focus on prayer when the pain level is at a 7 or 8. It seems like pain tends to push God out of one's focus. (A good friend shared with me sometime past that when you are hurting so bad and cannot pray, it is good to know you have friends who are praying for you.) It is times like this that His Spirit begins talking to my spirit. When that happens, it is almost exhilarating. There is also a sense of peace and assurance that is difficult to put into words. When the pain was so great that I could not pray, it seemed that He moved even closer.

I truly believe God is more interested in how I respond to pain more than the suffering it brings. I am still learning lessons on this journey. And, eventually, I guess it is not relevant whether I understand why I must endure this constant pain, I just need to remember He is there, loving and caring for me.

One of the most important things He has taught me is that He is leading me into a more profound relationship with Him. I believe beyond doubt that cancer has brought me closer to God! Most of my days are filled with a sense of tranquility and peace. Yes, the pain is definitely there, but so is God. He makes all the difference in my moods, attitudes, and perspectives.

Of the things I continually wrestle with, one is if I should fight to extend this life of pain? Does it, or is it helping someone else? The question sneaks up on me and asks, 'why should I keep on?' It is times like these I am reminded of Old Testament Job."

"Mortals have a limited life span. You've already decided how long we'll live-You set the boundary and no one can cross it." (Job 14:5 The Message). And then again in the Book of Psalms; " I will give thanks to You, for I am fearfully and wonderfully made; wonderful are Your works, And my soul knows it very well. My frame was not hidden from You, when I was made in secret, and skillfully wrought in the depths of the earth; Your eyes have seen my unformed substance; And in Your book were all written the days that were ordained for me, When as yet there was not one of them." (Psalm 139:14-16 NASB).

"It is times like these when I ask The Holy Spirit to help me to reject wrong thoughts. I guess I will just keep on keeping on until He is ready to take me home."

Keeping Bill's perspective in mind, let us spend just a few minutes and look at some who went through the pain and death struggle without God.

David Hume: Atheist philosopher famous for his religious skepticism, cried loud on his deathbed, "I am in flames."

Note the words of Napoleon Bonaparte, the French emperor who brought pain, suffering and death to millions simply to satisfy his selfish ambitions for world conquest. "I die before my time, and my body will be given back to the earth. Such is the fate of him who has been called The Great Napoleon. What an abyss between my deep misery and the eternal Kingdom of Christ!"

Then there is Joseph Stalin-Soviet revolutionary and politician. In a Newsweek interview with Svetlana, Stalin's daughter, she recounts his last moments: "My father died a difficult and horrible death... God grants an easy death only to the just. At what seemed the last moment, he suddenly opened his eyes and cast a glance over everyone in the room. It was a terrible glance, insane or perhaps angry. His left hand was raised, as though he were pointing to something above and bringing down a curse on us all. The gesture was full of menace... the next morning he was dead."

Finally, Anton Levey— Satanic Bible author and high priest of the Satanic worship religion. His dying words were, "Oh my, oh my, what have I done, there is something very wrong."

God has a plan for everyone's life. Occasionally, that plan leads through a tunnel of physical pain. For the one who has given their lives over to Jesus Christ, the pain is truly worth the reward at the end of the tunnel!

Before we move on to the next topic of pain, I thought it might be helpful for you to see the list of medications and procedures Bill has undertaken since his initial diagnosis.

The following are the scans and procedures that Bill had when first diagnosed. These were done to learn the type and location of the cancer, and to follow up on progress of the treatment given:

X-rays

Cat scans of chest, abdomen, and pelvis

Bone scans

Bone biopsy

PET scans

MRI

Kyphoplasty (insertion of cement into the spine for compression fractures to relieve pain and to stabilize the spine.)

Lab tests

CBC

PSA

PAIN-OPIODS

Oxycodone

Hydrocodone

Fentanyl

Morphine

DICLOFENAC-(anti- inflammatory)

NAUSEA (due to treatment/ pain medications)

Zofran

CONSTIPATION (due to pain medications)

Senokot-S (stool softener)

MiraLAX (laxative)

APPETITE/WEIGHT LOSS (appetite stimulate)

Megesterol

Modophinal

ANTI-TESTOSTERONE (stops the production of male hormone testosterone- - testosterone feeds prostate cancer cells)

Xtandia

Casodex

Abiraterone

Zoladex

CHEMOTHERAPY

Taxotere

BONE BUILDERS (slows the breakdown of bones; affects density and strength of the bones)

Zometa

HOT FLASHES (due to some of the anti-testosterone drugs)

Gabapentin

PREDNISONE (steroid used with one of the anti-testosterone drugs)

RADIATION (six treatments for pain control to spine)

Radium 223 and Olaparib (a clinical trial for patients resistant to previous treatments)

Pluvicto (radioactive drug that targets and prevents cells from duplicating)

OTHER MEDICATIONS

Levothyroxine (for hypothyroidism)

Omeprazole (for gastric reflux)

Lisinopril (for high blood pressure)

Lexapro (used for depression)

Yes, without a doubt, Bill has and is experiencing pain, suffering and the reality his body is approaching "shut-down-mode." He has never been one to complain, and even at this juncture of his life's journey, has traded the option of complaint for one of accepting and adapting. He shares that accepting and adapting gives him a myriad of options which complaining and lamenting ignore.

When asked to expand on this "accepting and adapting" option, Bill states: "Complaining is a dead-end street. It closes off the possibility of enjoying the daily times of joy and refreshment that often materialize." The visit of a friend, the meal dropped off because someone was thinking about you, and even the cool refreshment of his beloved milkshakes (Chocolate or Strawberry, no whipped cream or cherries)!

Another uncomfortable realization is that no one enjoys hearing continual complaints. Bill is training himself to reply, when asked "How are you feeling?" with the answer, "Alright." If the one asking the question decides to pursue it, he will acknowledge his daily difficulties, then attempt to change the subject. His words of explanation are, "complaining" never changes the pain level or current discomfort, and there is little most visitors can do to alleviate it, so why increase their burden with what they already know or suspect.

He is quick to explain it is different when the questions are coming from his health care professionals. Keeping them informed of his current condition allows them to evaluate and propose some possible avenues to pursue in managing his disease. His mantra, "Always be truthful with those who can actually make a difference, and the rest of the time just say, 'I'm alright!' They already know I am not always up to that standard, but it sure makes our time together much more enjoyable."

As we mentioned above, physical pain is something we have the unique ability to forget. You may always remember the "event" that caused the physical pain but will not re-visit the actual physical pain itself. Remembering the pain "causation" (or better called "pain memory") will never cause you to re-experience the actual physical pain.

There are some good physicians, scientists, and researchers who might disagree with my observation of physical pain. The point I want to make is (except in rare instances) physical pain is difficult at best to re-visit. I would like to highlight this difference to allow Bill to lead us into a different kind of pain discussion. A Pain that can be or become much more debilitating than actual physical pain.

"In 1980, the American Psychiatric Association added PTSD to the third edition of its Diagnostic and Statistical Manuel of Mental Disorders. Although controversial when first introduced, the PTSD diagnosis has filled an important gap in psychiatric theory and practice. From a historical perspective, the most significant change ushered in by the PTSD concept was the stipulation that the etiological agent was outside the individual (i.e., a traumatic event) rather than an inherent weakness (i.e., traumatic neurosis). The key to understanding the scientific basis and clinical expression is the concept of trauma."

(Matthew J Friedman, MD, PhD - - a brief history of the PTSD diagnosis)

As a workable definition of post-traumatic stress disorder (PTSD) and for the purpose of this discussion, let us adopt the above-mentioned concept. Anyone who has experienced an event or situation that was or is deeply emotional or psychologically stressful, suffers from a type of PTSD.

It would also seem logical to consider anyone who has been exposed to an event that is considered "traumatic" could and quite possibly will suffer from some degree of PTSD. We would be remiss if we did not observe that there will be those who have a higher threshold for trauma acceptance. Please note, this higher "trauma acceptance" threshold may help one personally, but can in some instances be construed as less caring or loving.

When we are the one who has a debilitating disease, or the caretaker of one who is experiencing such, it would seem wise to ask "why" we think and sometimes act the way we do. We can label it PTSD, extreme emotional distress, not accepting reality, or any other catchphrase we choose. The point is, contrary to what we have stated previously, there is a pain you will not only feel, but also remember, and there is nothing wrong with you when you do.

When you truly love someone, and they are hurting, it is normal and natural for you to vicariously enter into their hurt. As a caregiver, it is important to acknowledge and understand this because unless you do, you will push away a reality you should actually embrace. If you try to separate your emotions of impending loss from the actual reality facing you, you do yourself and the one you love a disservice.

It becomes a dis-service to the one who is dying or suffering because you cannot walk the road with them unless you take your shoes off (become tender and vulnerable). The chronically ill person wants you to not only acknowledge their suffering, pain, and sense of impending loss, but to do so authentically. The last thing they want is to be "pandered to."

When it comes to PTSD, both the chronically ill and close caregivers will experience this phenomenon. Understanding, accepting, and adapting to the situation will help everyone involved to be honest and authentic with one another.

Bill states: "When it comes to emotional pain, I believe there are demonic forces at work attempting to cause depression and self-defeat." He uses Ephesians Chapter Six as an antidote to the Devil's schemes of manipulation. Note the insight this passage provides:

"Finally, be strong in the Lord and in the strength of His might. Put on the full armor of God, that you may be able to stand firm against the schemes of the devil. For our struggle is not against flesh and blood but against the rulers, against the powers, against the world forces of this darkness, against the spiritual forces of wickedness in the heavenly places. Therefore, take up the full armor of God, that you may be able to resist in the evil day, and having done everything, to stand firm. Stand firm therefore, having girded your loins with truth, and having put on the breastplate of righteousness, and having shod your feet with the preparation of the Gospel of peace; in addition to all, taking up the shield of faith with which you will be able to extinguish all the flaming missiles of the evil one. And take the helmet of salvation, and the sword of the Spirit, which is the Word of God. With all prayer and petition pray at all times in the Spirit, and with this in view, be on the alert with all perseverance and petition for all the saints." (NASB)

For the believer, it is important to remember the forces of evil will come at you even harder and more consistently when physical, emotional, and psychological pain are present. The devil's desire is to, at the least make you feel vulnerable, defenseless, and weak. At the most, he would like you to curse God for your physical condition and make all those around you suffer spiritually, and emotionally as well.

It might actually help for the Christ centered believer to remember, "This world is not my home!" We should, of course, be good stewards of our environment and the earthly gifts God has bestowed upon us. Conversely at the same time, we should also remember the things of this present world will one day have no influence upon us. Until that day dawns, let us "be steadfast, immovable, always abounding in the work of the Lord, knowing that your toil is not in vain in the Lord." (I Corinthians 15:58- NASB)

UPDATE AUGUST 24TH 2022

As most of you know, Sharon changed her mortal relationship with Jesus from this earth to an immortal perfect one in heaven on May 2nd. That is a double-edged sword. She is enjoying each moment now beyond what we can possibly imagine. (We Can Only Imagine).

The other side of the sword is the overwhelming sadness and grief I am learning to live with. I had no idea something like that could hurt so much. I have taught Sunday School and Bible classes for over five decades, so I believe I have a pretty good idea of what is happening.

I have the peace of the Father with me. I can't explain or describe it, but it is real, even in my deepest sorrow and depression. PTL

Thank you for your love, prayers, and support during this time. Many of you made a memorial contribution in Sharon's name. Over $1,000.00 was given.

Here is the "Cliff Notes" update on me. I have had this cancer for seven years and according to the oncologists, I should not have survived beyond five years. I have.

I have experienced numerous lessons on learning about God, heaven, love, pain, etc. I would not trade these lessons for anything! (That is not to say I want to do it again.)

My pain levels from the tumors on my bones are getting worse. Fentanyl patches were being given in stronger doses, and then God answered prayer in a way I would never have thought of.

I think it was Bill Gaither who wrote a song that says, "God is always working, never stops working." Sometimes I can't see Him working and that is very frustrating. In this situation the doctors were continuing to increase the amount of pain medications with no real hope in sight except for perhaps me being confined to constant mobility help. Now at this time, unbeknownst to me or those in Topeka, my physician (anesthesia) trained son was talking to his friend and peer who specializes in spine pain management. The result is now I have an intrathecal pain pump inserted in my spine that has reduced my pain levels to the low 5's. I praise God and am going to have to continue working on faith when nothing seems to be happening.

That is an update on my cancer. The cancer is active again now at an increased rate. I am being referred to Kansas University

Medical Center Research for a second opinion. I may do another clinical trial, but I need more details about potential side effects. Then I think "I would not have had the cancer drugs of today if no one had volunteered," so I will probably do it. If it does not work, then I have an estimated 18 to 24 months to live. As I have written in the past, early on in this cancer journey God told me I would not die from cancer in 2015, and that I would die when my work on this earth is done, so I don't really give it a lot of thought. I must admit, going home to my real country sure sounds good some days.

Well, I am rambling. Probably one of the most important lessons I have learned in this journey is the power of intercessory prayer. I have always known intercessory prayer works, but to experience it in your life year after year is nothing short of amazing. Since Sharon started intercessory prayer, we have had over 13,000 Caring Bridge responses. She and I both know and felt it during her terrible last year as she was in and out of the hospital, and I was getting worse day by day. I want to say "Thank You" to each who has prayed for us both, and tell you how much it meant, more than you could ever know.

3 THE CANCER JOURNEY BEGINS

Bill was diagnosed with stage 4 Prostate Cancer on October 23, 2015. This is also the date of his birthday. The following is Bill's personal description of those early days of diagnosis and treatment. Please keep in mind, what you are about to read has to do with his personal journey after initial diagnosis.

"I am a very private person; however, I felt it might be beneficial for some who have or will travel this same road to share some of my experiences on this cancer journey. My prayer is that it will help anyone going through a very difficult trial to know that Jesus is real, and that He really cares about you and will give you strength when you need it most. It is my story and, like all others, is custom-made by God for me. I believe He has a 'custom' story for everyone who will listen to the storyteller.

For years, I have taught that God loves you when you are going through a trial. Boy was I ever about to test that truth.

As stated above, I was diagnosed with stage 4 Prostate Cancer on my birthday, October 23rd, 2015. At the time of diagnosis, the cancer had left the prostate and metastasized to all my bones. It was especially severe in the spine and lower back. It is incurable.

This cancer journey began after what was a run of great health. I had not experienced anything more than a minor cold or flu bug for almost 40 years. Then in September 2015, I had what my primary care doctor thought was an infection. After two rounds of antibiotics, he referred me to an Infectious Disease Doctor. He did not like what he saw and ordered an MRI. When he got the results, he immediately referred me to an oncologist. All my bones, especially my spine and lower back 'lit up like a Christmas tree' on the MRI results.

The next step was a bone scan and biopsy. Now, let me tell you, that was another new experience. I had never before been 'put to sleep' in an operating room. Those results came back and were not good. More tests were needed for confirmation.

After that came CT scans and x-rays. They confirmed the MRI and biopsy results. It was in fact stage 4 Prostate Cancer."

We are going to pause Bill's narrative to interject some questions posed to him, which you may be wondering about.

Question:

Bill, what were your initial thoughts and reaction to your diagnosis?

"Well, first there was some confusion. The only thing I knew about cancer was what I had picked up through various conversations. I do remember there was no sense of apprehension or real fear at the time. (Those reactions and emotions would attempt to attack at a later time)."

Question:

How did you break the news to your wife and family?

"Sharon had an idea something was wrong. A wife's intuition, perhaps. I think her first clue was when I returned from an afternoon of fishing and could not climb the bank and get back to my car without help. I do remember when the oncologist told us that death was imminent, she did not show any great emotion. Eventually, the oncologist requested a meeting with the entire family to discuss my situation. It was there that they were advised about my condition. I vividly remember each of them saying they would "walk with me and that God was with me."

Question:

How did you let your friends and others know about your condition?

"It was a slow, day by day process. I was leading a Sunday School Class and a Small Group at the time. It did not take long for the word to get around after talking to both of those groups. I do remember Sharon used Caring Bridge to communicate with others."

Question:

I have heard that some people go through a period of denial after diagnosis. Did you experience anything like that?

"No, not anything that I would call denial, or even sadness. Let me be clear though, I was never, nor am I presently 'cavalier' about my situation. I know I am terminal and that this cancer will eventually take my life. I do have a sense of peace though that always seems to linger in the background of my days."

Question:

Ok, no real fears or denial, what did you feel?

"Well, as I stated earlier, at first, there was confusion, and a lack of understanding. Maybe a good word to use here might be 'apprehension,' not so much about my future, but about the process of treatment, expense, Insurance, lifestyle changes and things of that nature."

Question:

What was your attitude and approach to God about your diagnosis?

"I have never, to this point, ever had a 'Why Me' moment with Him. I think my overall thought and prayer process has been how I now see God. I used to think and react more from an outside perspective. Now I constantly see myself as in His presence. It is a little difficult to describe. Peace and acceptance are the words that come immediately to mind. I know I used to teach on the 'fact' level. Today, I would have to say it is much more about relationship. I can say undoubtedly, I 'feel' and 'experience' God's unconditional love. I am also convinced He is more interested in my response to Him than about any questions of why."

Question:

Has the Devil tried to jump on your back or intimidate you?

"It seems like he tries to bring the past up rather frequently. Especially the dark things in my past. Times I have disappointed myself and others. Times I have fallen so short of His best for me. The times I could have done better but decided to take the lower road. It is times like this that I find great joy and pleasure in reminding him that God has forgiven and forgotten all those things through Jesus' atonement on the Cross. I love to quote him Romans 8:1, 'There is now no condemnation for those who are in Christ Jesus.' Let me also add, I have never doubted my salvation experience. In fact, it is that very experience which gives me daily assurance and joy. I delight in quoting Psalm 103:1-2 and 8-12. "Bless the Lord, O my soul, and all that is within me, bless His holy name. Bless the Lord, O my soul, and forget none of His benefits. The Lord is compassionate and gracious, slow to anger and abounding in loving kindness. He will not always strive with us; Nor will He keep His anger forever. He has not dealt with us according to our sins, nor rewarded us according to our iniquities. For as high as the heavens are above the earth, so great is His loving kindness toward those who fear Him. As far as the east is from the west, so far, has He removed our transgressions from us."

I will have to admit that there have been times when God seemed so very near, and times so far away. I know this is because I am human, and these are indeed just 'feelings' and not 'fact.' They do spring up now and then though.'

You will remember we left Bill's narrative of events after the MRI and biopsy had confirmed the cancer diagnosis.

Let's pick up where we left off.

"The following Tuesday, I went into surgery again. This time it was to put a port into my chest. This is a small device inserted to provide access for chemo or drawing of blood. For the next year and beyond, it was used to give chemotherapy infusions. That sure beat getting 'stabbed' each week.

When I first met the Oncologist, I was in a wheelchair and experiencing some rather dark days. Not of depression or anything like that but just being too sick to even walk. I looked and felt terrible. Later he would tell us that I was in the valley of the shadow of death. I was so bad he did not think he could even treat me, but he would try.

I could not pray or read scripture. When you are really sick, you can't pray, read scripture, or focus on much of anything. I was confused and somewhat concerned about what was happening to me.

It was in the midst of this very dark time that a remarkable thing happened. It was about two weeks after the initial diagnosis. I got out of bed about 2:30 in the morning, not really knowing why. I sat in my favorite La-Z-Boy chair and just tried to relax. There, the Lord Jesus Christ sat next to me and said in effect, 'You will not die of this cancer at this time. When you have done all the work I have for you, then I'll call you home.'

This was not a physical Jesus, nor an audible voice, but it was as real as anything I have ever experienced. I believed Him and have never had a severely depressed day. I have had plenty of miserable days after chemotherapy, but no deep depression days.

This is where I think faith plays a part. A simple way to explain faith is a 'sixth spiritual sense.' Our five senses, touch, sight, hearing, smell, and taste make up what is all around us. When we see a beautiful sunset, our 'sight' sense kicks in. When we smell a juicy T-bone on the grill, our 'smell' sense activates.

It is the same with faith. God is always all around and near us. Through the Holy Spirit, our 'sixth sense' is activated, and we become aware of His presence and promises, just as if we experienced Him within our five senses.

The Lord Jesus Christ is a remarkable physician. Hundreds of intercessors and His miraculous power has kept me going to date. He also used an outstanding cancer center and staff at St. Francis Hospital. Yes, God can and does use prayer, health care professionals and modern technology to see His purposes accomplished.

The Lord Jesus Christ either allowed or caused the stage 4 Prostate Cancer. It is incurable and, in a few years, may very well kill me. The key lesson here is that God is always with us in our discomfort.

If I had never contracted this cancer, my walk with the Lord would have remained on a plateau. This disease brought home to me a new and more profound relationship with Jesus. When the pain, fatigue and overall 'bum' feelings come, I am learning to thank God for His provision and care. James 1:2-4 has been one of my go to verses!

'Consider it pure joy, my brothers, whenever you face trials of many kinds because you know that the testing of your faith develops perseverance. Perseverance must finish its work so that you may be mature and complete, not lacking anything.' (James1:2)

Claiming the power of these verses has been a great teacher for me. Admittedly, I don't always understand what is going on, but Philippians 4:5-7 has become an incredibly powerful truth for me to claim when those uncomfortable days occur.

'The Lord is near. Do not be anxious about anything, but in everything, by prayer and petition with thanksgiving, present your requests to God. And the peace of God, which transcends all understanding, will guard your hearts and your minds in Christ Jesus.'

Chemotherapy is difficult. You are infused with chemicals that kill cancer cells, while at the same time having some very real side effects. They tend to make you very sore and fatigued. It is a drudgery that must be endured. On the positive side, I have learned to attach new meanings to procedures. For those not familiar with the chemotherapy routine, allow me to share with you mine. (Please keep in mind, each person's 'prescription' will be somewhat different).

Daily-Casodex and Prednisone pill combination kills new cancer cells before they grow. Prednisone is like putting the Casodex on steroids.

Weekly Taxotere infusions at the cancer center. It stops existing live cancer cells before they grow anymore. I had 18 of these; the maximum amount you can have. We finished this phase in April and the hair and nails are slowly growing back. Not all the hair --- some miracles just won't happen!

Monthly is an infusion called Zometa or Zoledronic acid. It reduces bone destruction and helps existing damaged bones rebuild. I will take about two years of this infusion. Likewise, it is also called 'chemo brain.'

Quarterly Zolodex is administered. It is a shot received in the stomach that reduces cancer causing hormones and prevents new cancer cells from growing by starving them to death. I will have this quarterly shot for the rest of my life.

As I mentioned before, all chemotherapy drugs have side effects. Taxotere causes hair and nails to fall out. Zometa causes the most pain in the muscles and joints. Zolodex causes numerous hot flashes along with a lot of muscle and bone pain. Needless to say, this combined with Zometa makes for a difficult few days.

Other prescriptions are Hydrocodone for pain. It works, but also causes that 'chemo brain' effect. I use the term "chemo brain" in regard to memory problems and thinking processes. Prednisone and Zolodex cause weight gain. My wife Sharon says my weight gain is primarily because of my craving for cookies and milk, but I am sure she is absolutely mistaken! I also take Gabapentin which helps control hot flashes, but it can cause memory loss and make you kind of goofy. And there are, of course, OTCs (over the counter) of Ibuprofen, Sudafed and Benadryl.

I am attaching a new meaning to pain (there is a whole chapter dealing with this subject later). I know it will be chronic. It is a core truth I have had to accept. Alongside that truth is an even deeper 'core' truth; God deeply loves me and cares about what happens to me. However, as I have mentioned before, He cares even more about how I respond to what happens to me.

I am learning how to attach new meaning to 'scars.' Different levels of pain seem to stimulate a more in-depth understanding of why God is allowing this disease. He could have either stopped it in the beginning or never let it occur at all. He chose to do neither. That said, I would not have had the closeness to Him that I now know exists without the disease. I was not in danger of 'losing my salvation,' but like many of us, I was pretty comfortable in my 'walk.' Apparently, God knew I needed a wake-up call if He was going to be able to bless me more. I must admit, I am still working on that one.

For me, I needed to slow down and get to a closer relationship with Him. I had what, I thought, was a pretty good walk, but He had something different and better in mind.

There is one good thing about cancer. You have a lot of time on your hands as you don't feel like going anywhere. Eventually, I was able to underline hundreds of meaningful scripture verses from Genesis to Revelation. I love to learn new things. I have always enjoyed studying scripture. This disease has brought about a much deeper appreciation of God's Word. Numerous of them have had new meanings that brings me closer to God.

There are also some good things I am discovering on this journey. I never realized how many Christian friends Sharon and I have. It is quite humbling. We have had prayer support from our Sunday School class; Small Group; family, friends near Topeka and missionaries all over the world.

We have been overwhelmed by the outpouring of love through cards, meals, and personal visits. The downside is I am really putting on the pounds!

The journey is not over. The restoring of the damaged bones will go on, and prevention of new cancer cells will be needed until I die. The process goes on and faith continues to grow.

My Oncologist has retired. The new Oncologist has moved my monthly infusions to quarterly, along with reducing some prescriptions. Healing seems to be working.

I am wrestling with what new study groups I should work in. It is unclear. Perhaps I should process it like the song says: 'If just a cup of water I give you, then just a cup of water is all I demand.'"

UPDATE DECEMBER 28TH 2022

The words of the song "Through It All" are certainly applicable to 2022. Through it all the Lord Jesus Christ has been with me. I can't explain it, but His presence was and is so real, even in the times of the fiercest storms.

The major one was the death of Sharon on May 2nd. After 56 years of marriage my treasure went home to be with The Lord. I had no idea how much this would actually hurt. I attended the "Grief Share" course, and it was helpful, but did not remove the sense of loss and sorrow. It still hurts as I attempt to share this with you, yet maybe not quite as severe or as often. I am 79 years old, and perhaps I can also go home soon.

When I was first diagnosed with cancer 7 plus years ago, the Lord told me "When your work is done, I will take you home." Apparently, He still has something for me to do! I did retire after teaching Sunday School for over five decades. (Maybe I will start that again).

The second largest trial was the death of my brother Bob. I am not sure he ever made a profession of faith. Maybe he did, I just do not know and try not to obsess about it.

The number three trial had to do with my cancer. Early in the year it started to get really active again. It was determined that the hormonal drugs were no longer working, as the cancer had found a way of working around them. My Topeka Oncologists started me on another expensive drug, which did not have any effect either. My KU Oncologist tried an equally expensive drug which also had no effect on my cancer. The decision is for me to now go to KUMC once a month for 223 radiation infusions. They seem to be helping. The doctor asked if I would be willing to do a clinical trial with an experimental drug. I said sure, someone had to do trials for the drugs I was now receiving, so why should I do any different. I started this new drug in October, and it seems to be helping. The only side effect of any consequence is fatigue, which is a small price to pay for feeling better. As a positive outcome, the drug costs $25,000 a month and the National Cancer Institute pays for it. If the trial goes well they may pay for it for the rest of my life.

Pain levels were not under control, so my Topeka Oncologist set me up with a palliative pain control team. We tried increased hydrocodone and then increased fentanyl. There was minimal relief at best. My Physician son David, set me up with a pain doctor in Wichita, Kansas. I had an intrathecal pain pump with a bonus inserted surgically. This has been a great help!

The lumbar pain is still quite severe. The spine doctor believes I probably have a fractured disc. We are waiting to get an MRI and then decide to go from there.

In September I had a bad fall and went to the ER. I had a slight concussion, six stitches in my lower lip, a possible cracked wrist, and multiple bruises.

My whole year was not all gloom and doom. Yes, I did have depression issues as well as feelings of loneliness, but Jesus Christ and God's Word were always there. I am learning to trust, especially when I don't understand what is happening. I am sure my "lessons" are not over. I just hope 2023 has easier lessons!

Friends and care givers were and are a key part of my learning experience. I love them more than I can put into words. Sharon was a lot better at that than I am. My family has been extra sensitive and supportive.

I am a big believer in intercessory prayer as I saw it work more times than I can count in 2022.

On a lighter note, I did get a dog. She is a 4-month-old Labradoodle. She is not housebroken yet but will be very soon. One additional note: I bought a Cadillac I had always wanted.

4 A CANDID LOOK AT THE PROCESS

"There is a land that is fairer than day, and by faith we can see it a-far

For the Father waits over the way, to prepare us a dwelling place there.

We shall sing on that beautiful shore, The melodious songs of of the blest,

and our spirits shall sorrow no more, not a sigh for the blessing of rest.

To our bountiful Father above, we will offer our tribute of praise,

For the glorious gift of His love, and the blessings that hallow Our days.

In the sweet by-and by, we shall meet on that beautiful shore."

Most are aware of the often-used phrase, "we all want to go to heaven, we just don't like the process." Seldom do we fear the future, we just fear what we do not know about the future.

So, let's look at the process of getting to heaven.

Most would agree we need a process to arrive at anything of value. It was W. Edwards Deming, an American professor, author, and consultant who said, "Don't inspect the product, inspect the process."

The product (heaven) is not up for discussion at this point. Let's just assume a majority believe there is life after life. Remember, we are approaching this reality we call the end of life, death, or perhaps even going home, from a faith-based perspective.

Whether death comes suddenly or after a long battle with illness, there are certain areas of our journey which needs to be addressed and taken care of before that moment of transition. Addressing these areas of necessity will make it easier on your family and those left behind. Going through these steps will accomplish two distinct things. First, it will provide a guide of your wishes after your departure and second, it will give you a sense of peace and accomplishment.

With that as a starting point, let's explore five points of the process.

(The following is intended as a guide only, and not to be construed as to giving medical or legal advice.)

Gather important information in one place and make it accessible to a trusted family member or friend. Things like bank accounts and investments, birth certificate, social security card, military records, wills and trusts, insurance policies, mortgage documents and any other pertinent information that pertains to you. Once gathered, store them in a safe place where that trusted family member or friend can access them easily. You might want to think about including the location of these documents in your will and in any other instructional documents you want to leave behind.

Start now and create a Living Will. This is a legal document that makes known your wishes for medical treatment if you are unable to cognitively make those decisions for yourself. This document allows your caregivers and loved ones to give you the very best care without having to address critical questions at an extremely stressful time. Make sure you include things such as life-saving measures and other medical treatments you want for yourself.

In this advanced directive, you should think through and include things like if you want to be placed on life support and the kind of pain management you want and are comfortable with. Be as specific as possible, so there is no question or confusion about your wishes. If you have a lawyer that you routinely use, they can help you in the preparation of your wishes. That said, you really don't need an attorney to prepare an advanced directive. This is something you can do on your own; however, make sure it is properly signed and witnessed. Having a notary involved when witnessing your documents adds to its credibility. At least three people should have a copy of this document: your doctor, a trusted loved one, and the intended executor of your estate.

If you have specific wishes for what should happen to your body after death, such as donating organs, cremation, burial, or if you want to donate your body to a medical school or research hospital, be sure to notate these instructions clearly.

Preparing an advanced directive (living will) will give you some peace of mind, knowing your wishes will be carried out when the time comes. As already mentioned, it also takes a lot of decision-making stress off those who want to do the best for you.

Another important thing for you to do is to have a will prepared. Again, you do not necessarily need an attorney to do this for you, but it is advisable. A will is a legal document which gives direction about how you want your belongings to be taken care of after you have moved into your new home (Heaven). It is advised to not put this off for another day. In the event of your death without a will, the State can and will often decide how your possessions will be divided.

When you write your will, there are some things you need to make sure you include. First, you will need to appoint an executor of your estate. It would be wise to get this person's permission for such a position. This is the person(s) who will be responsible for carrying out your wishes. Make sure you list all your assets and how you want them to be distributed.

Keep your will up to date. Things change with time, and so may your assets and wishes. Revisit your will anytime there is a major life change. (Marriage, children, obtaining new or distributing prior assets etc.)

There is something known as a Codicil to a will, which many States will accept. This can be a handwritten and signed declaration and directions for all your possessions. (If you are going to do this, it might be advisable to just write a new will.) When my mother-in-law passed, we found her will in the family safe deposit box in their local bank. Inside the written will were several tablet-sized pages which she wanted added to her final wishes. I remember this distinctively because she noted she wanted me to get all her pots, pans, and cookbooks. (We both enjoyed cooking, and she had some incredible pots and pans which I had admired many times.)

Another step in preparation is to appoint a power of attorney. This is a legal document which gives the person of your choosing the authority to make decisions on your behalf if you are unable to do so. You can appoint a power of attorney for health care decisions, as well as financial direction, or you can separate the two and have a power of attorney for just medical decisions, and another for financial direction.

When appointing a power of attorney (POA) insure they are someone you trust unquestionably. Furthermore, it is wise to appoint someone who lives close by, as they may need to act quickly on your behalf. Another thought for you to consider is to appoint an alternate power of attorney in case your primary choice is unable or unavailable.

Make sure you check your state laws regarding wills, trust, and especially your power of attorney designation. Each State has their own regulations concerning these areas, and you will want to comply.

One final note regarding POA's: There are two different designations. They are called durable and non-durable. (Actually, there is another called "springing" but rarely is used or needed.) A durable POA stays in effect even if you become unable to make your own decisions. A non-durable Power of attorney only applies when you can still make decisions for yourself. It ceases to have authority if you become incapacitated (senility, coma, dementia etc.).

While making preparations, something you may want to consider is purchasing life insurance or setting aside a certain amount of your assets to take care of costs associated with caring out your final wishes. This helps to relieve the often-abrupt necessity of requiring funds for final wishes and directives.

When looking at the above-mentioned items, an option you could consider is to have an attorney draw up a revocable trust. A revocable trust (also known as a Revocable Living Trust) is a changeable legal agreement where a trustee holds assets for you and beneficiaries while you are alive. A revocable living trust can help your estate and heirs avoid the hassle and costs of probate.

And now for a difficult decision for you to make regarding your passing into that new residence in the heavenly realms: Do you want to opt for cremation or burial? Do you want to have a funeral or a memorial?

Whatever decision you make, leave a copy with the funeral home of your choosing, as well as a copy with that trusted individual.

Buy your burial plot now. If you wait until your passing, it will quite possibly be pricier. A wise man said, "They are not making any more dirt." So, take care of what you can while you can!

You may want to think about how you would want any memorial gifts used. This will take an enormous burden off those who are left behind.

A funeral normally includes several elements which a memorial would not. For instance, if you decide on the funeral route, a decision on a casket, burial site, and funeral preparations required by law for funeral directors to follow must be considered.

In contrast, a memorial service is usually selected when the body has been cremated. It often includes the same elements of the funeral service, without the body being present. One of the advantages of a memorial service is that there is no time limit involved. Most States will require a funeral service be conducted with 7–10 days of the person's passing.

Regardless of the direction you decide upon, planning in these areas is a wise course of action. In one sense, it is a way of telling those who have been left behind that you were thinking of them and attempting to relieve as much stress as possible before going home.

Another area which is typically overlooked in the digital age is to make allowance for the following to be taken care of in the event of your death. Online banking and financial records, social media accounts, e-mail addresses, digital photos and other online accounts need to be addressed. In addition, all passwords should be updated and monitored for at least 12–18 months. This could be called digital estate management.

Finally, let your family and loved ones know of the preparations you have decided upon. This will quite possibly include a difficult and uncomfortable conversation. Do not neglect this part of your plan, though. So much can be lost simply because those left behind did not know where to find your final plans and wishes.

BILL'S UPDATE APRIL 15TH 2023

Thank you for friendships and intercessory prayers over these past years. These past few months have been pretty busy. I had kyphoplasty surgery (a procedure to treat compression fractures), two epidurals, an addition of a palliative care team to help pain management and completed a Comrade trial procedure. This was a clinical trial administered by The Kansas University Medical Center, one of the premier cancer and treatment centers in America. It was a six-month study, and depending on the results, three options would be made available to me.

The first was if the trial showed positive results. If so, we would continue with monthly "Olaparid" pills and stop the monthly radiation with 223 radium isotopes. This would be a good outcome.

The second would be if the treatment did not work or show any significant signs of success. Then the study would stop, and I would begin Hospice care.

Yet another option would be to take a new drug called "Pluvicto." It consists of six treatments at a cost of around $45,000 each. That is a no starter!

Last week we had our meeting. The doctor said I was no longer a candidate for any of the above options. The reason was because the tests came back and said things seemed to be "in control." They told me that means I could live a few months, an extended amount of time, or die tomorrow. (Actually, this was good news!)

I am trusting God the Father, Son and Holy Spirit to work all things according to His purpose. Next up is all the bone scans, CTs and MRIs which are done quarterly.

I had to give my Labradoodle puppy away. She was tripping me too often and it was just too unsafe. I still miss Sharon immensely, and no doubt will until I see her again in heaven. In the meantime, thank you loving and kind family and friends. My "go to" verses for 2023 so far are Philippians 3:12-16.

It has been a little over a month since my first infusion of Pluvicto. The results have been very mixed. Time will make things clearer perhaps.

The Holy Spirit continues to give me more insights about God, relationships with God and insightful truths about heaven.

If I were to dare give any advice about how to handle a cancer diagnosis, it would be, "don't run from it but embrace it."

One of the most important things you need to do is to make sure you have a close relationship with the Lord Jesus Christ. Take my word for it, you will need Him!

Next, have a good caregiver. In my case I had the best. My wife Sharon was wonderful for the first few years. Then things changed for her. She had several chronic illnesses. Eventually our roles reversed, and I became her primary caregiver, taxi driver, and overall encourager. Never in my wildest dreams would I have guessed that I would soon use those learned skills for myself. It was May 2nd, 2022, when her faith was rewarded, and Jesus took her home.

5 BE HONEST WITH YOURSELF

It has been said, "We begin to die the moment we're born." There is a day coming when we will all breathe our last breath and then make that transition into the next realm of life. It is possible for you to ignore this truth, but I believe you will be doing yourself a terrible injustice if you decide to ignore reality. Remember "Reality" is an undefeated champion!

The choices we make today become unchangeable when we die. Many of those decisions will determine how and where we will spend eternity. In reality there are only two eternal destinations: a wonderful heaven or a terrible hell! We are not alone in having to make this sort of decision. All humanity will and must deal with this very aspect of their individual future and eternal destiny.

It should not be considered morbid or unthinkable to accept the fact that we will not live forever in this present world. Things will someday change, and so will we! I don't think we should spend an inordinate amount of time dwelling on the issue, but neither should we ignore it!

I would like to suggest that an important part of the process of living in this present world is knowing where you are going to spend eternity in the future. We could even look at this as part of our "estate planning." By its very definition, this is and should be a spiritual decision, for there is a part of our developed being which will never die.

The part of our true essence which never terminates is often referred to as our soul, or our spirit. Some might even refer to it as conscious, or the real you. Regardless, it seems reasonable to assume we are more than just a body floating through a journey called life.

Most would attest we are far more than just what we see reflected in the mirror. There seems to be a dynamic about "us" which we can never truly fathom or explain outside of the spiritual. How can we begin to explain where our feelings come from? Where do our emotions originate? Where are things such as love and hate born? How and where are good and evil conceived? Where and how do our thoughts originate?

To be fair, some would say all of the above originate in the mind. Without question your brain (mind) is a mysterious and wonderful tool, but that is all it really is --- a tool. Something is feeding the mind and thinking processes. For those who might legitimately question this, how would we explain "telling" the mind (brain) what to process or think about?

Allow me to suggest the following for your consideration. When you use the term "I" when speaking to or about yourself, who is the "I?" If you were to say it is my mind speaking, who is the "my?" It seems we have no logical way to explain such conundrums unless we allow that personhood is more than just a body with a mind controlling all aspects of its generated being.

As mentioned above, we describe this part of our "being" with different titles. Could we agree for the purpose of understanding and illustration, that there is a part of our created being which operates separately from our mind and body? If so, could we call this what most Theologians describe as "spirit?"

H. Orton Wiley relates it this way in his work "Introduction To Christian Theology," stating, "The word soul as used here refers to the immaterial entity, marked by sensation, feeling and will, which characterized this new order of creation. The word is not synonymous with the word 'spirit' which is used to indicate man's immaterial nature in its relations to deity and the moral order." (Pg138)

For clarification, the soul functions (sensation, feelings and will) are the part of our being which will one day terminate at death of the body. The spirit functions, the immaterial which deals with spirituality and morality, will live on forever.

Theologically, the "spirit" is the repository of all things which deal with morality. Your mind (brain) processes what is born out of the spirit. If thoughts and actions have no moral implications, then it stands to reason they also have no eternal ramifications. But, if a thought or action has a moral basis, they also have eternal consequences.

The question we should then wrestle with is this: What becomes of the eternal destiny of the spirit? The real you. The "conscious" you. The part of you which will never die because your spirit has immortality. I highlight this because the choices we make on this side of eternity will determine the destiny of the spirit.

So, in light of what we know about our spirit, why is this of any real importance? I would suggest its importance is to be reminded that the part of your cognitive being (spirit) will never cease to exist. Because it lives immortal, we should give careful attention to its dwelling place in eternity!

This brings us face to face to the eternal core question about our earthly choices. Note, we are free moral agents. Thus, we have the God given right and responsibility of choice. To put it another way, we have been given the wonderful privilege of determining where our spirit (the real cognitive you) will live for eternity. Think about this; you get to choose to live in a place created by The Creator God, or in a place created for those who choose to deny His very existence. Without doubt, this is quite a responsibility.

The apostle John, the only one of the original disciples of Jesus who lived into old age said, "For God so loved the world that He gave his only begotten Son, that whosoever believes in Him should not perish, but have eternal life." (John 3:16 NASB).

Friend, choose wisely, for your destiny is in your hands, and the decisions made in your spirit will have eternal consequences. Plainly said, the only way to heaven is to believe that God sent His Son to die and to pay the penalty for your sins, and for you to accept His forgiveness. The good news is your penalty has been paid. The question you must answer is, "Have you accepted His forgiveness?" Unfortunately, if you choose to go your own way, you will be required to pay your own debt. Please understand you cannot pay your way into God's eternal home, only Jesus can and will do that for you.

Allow me to suggest you pray in and through your "spirit" this simple prayer; "God, I know I have sinned and do not deserve to live with You in heaven for eternity. I realize my sins and transgressions separate me from You. I acknowledge You sent Jesus into this world I am living in to pay the price for my sins. This moment I accept your forgiveness through Your Son's payment of my debt. I accept Jesus as my Savior and say Thank You God! In Jesus Name I pray, Amen."

At this moment you are as ready as you will ever be for your transition into the next realm of living. Congratulations, you have been and are being honest with yourself.

BILL'S UPDATE SEPTEMBER 11ᵀᴴ 2023

I had my six month visit with my primary care doctor. He believes from what he can see that there is no need for hospice yet. So far, three doctors (Primary Care, Oncology, and Hospice) now say there is no need for hospice. For this I am grateful.

My Primary Care Doctor is treating me for very low thyroid, with Levothyroxine as the drug of choice. He has also ordered an MRI for a possible torn rotator cuff. (I sure would like to talk to the biblical "Job" and get some useful pointers! (Ha-ha))

Jesus of the Trinity will one day take my mortal body and CHANGE it into a glorious body like His. Just as we have a lot of the physical traits of our parents, so we also have many of our heavenly Father's spiritual traits. As a child of God, I will one day have a new powerful and glorious body of immortality. Sobering thought, isn't it? Philippians 3:20-21 says, "He will take our weak mortal bodies and change them into glorious bodies like His own, using the same power with which He will bring everything under His control."

I am wrestling now with whether I should continue with medication LU177. I am not sure it is helping, but then it is not designed to do that. I have already taken the last and strongest cancer Medication that will kill cancer cells. LU177 (also called Lutenium and Plavicto) is the last drug the FDA has approved. Its only purpose is to prolong life.

The other issue is as I have stated previously, and am convinced, The Father said He will take me home when my work is done. I, at times ask myself, did I misunderstand?

I am getting worse at what I believe to be an accelerating pace. This type of cancer normally kills in 3-5 years after diagnosis. I will soon be starting my 9th year. God has taught me a lot of things, and it seems I have shared so little. My goal is to do better in this department. Eight years ago, I was able to walk, mow grass, go fishing and attend to many of the things around the house. Over the next few years, I found using a cane occasionally to be a help. Before long, it was two canes, and now a walker. I don't know what is next.

When it comes to family, be sensitive to their feelings. Each loved one is going to struggle with your disease differently. Patience would be a good discipline to practice. It took two of my three sons quite some time before they could or would say the C word.

Learn to value and appreciate your health care providers, as well as your close friends. Remember, because they care about you, they will also struggle in their own private way.

Loneliness is a major issue. Yes, I know Jesus is with me, but we don't necessarily talk the way we will when we arrive in heaven. So many days I go without talking, except to my son Jon who checks on me every day. Two men my age have recently come on the scene and that is taking a bit of the daily loneliness away.

More musings on health, medications, closeness of the different persons of the Trinity, and anything else that crosses my mind will come later.

6 A WONDERFUL RESOURCE - - HOSPICE

The following information is not to be construed as definitive in any aspect. It is solely offered as a guideline of "thought processes" concerning end of life care. It has been culled from content available through "the fair use Index" of available sources.

In the early 1980's, a new concept of end-of-life care was being developed. Instead of just focusing on the physical, it was developed to be more holistic as a person transitioned from curative care to end of life care.

Hospice care is a type of health care that focuses on the entire person, not just the physical aspect. It prioritizes comfort and quality of life by minimizing physical pain while at the same time acknowledging other non-curative needs a patient has.

These services are designed as a specialized form of medical care that seeks to provide comfort and maintain a patient's quality of life for those facing a life-limiting illness, disease, or terminal condition.

Generally, they will include comprehensive, interdisciplinary care from a team of professionals and volunteers. The care can involve physicians, case management nurses, home health aides, certified medical social workers, chaplains, and various other volunteers.

Care is normally available 24 hours a day, including weekends and holidays.

Hospice seeks to manage pain and other physical symptoms. The care provided focuses on comfort and quality of life. Hospice nurses and other personnel work with patients and their loved ones to determine the degree of pain management needed, thus insuring the best response to treatment.

One of the advantages of choosing this kind of specialized care is it can often avoid unwanted hospitalizations, medical treatments, and procedures. The goal of the care-giving team is to support the patient and their family members' wishes.

Hospice services normally provide help with medical and non-medical needs. In addition, it helps address the spiritual and psychological needs of patients and their caregivers. Spiritual advisors, grief counselors, and social workers trained in addressing emotional needs are often offered as needed or requested.

Home or impatient care is commonly offered in this unique setting. Because hospice care aims to maintain quality of life, many of these organizations offer care in the comfort of the patients' personal home. When this is the case, they will deliver any specialized equipment or medication required directly to the patient's home.

A potential disadvantage of choosing such care can arise due to restrictions placed on the various aspects of treatment. Under the Medicare hospice benefit, a hospice receives a flat per-day amount of money from which all medical expenses must be paid. This can at times become problematic.

Denial of some diagnostic tests might occur, such as blood work and X-rays. Even if requested by the patient's attending physician, the cost of these tests often becomes the financial responsibility of the hospice agency. Because the tests can be quite expensive at times and might not be beneficial, these agencies often forgo approval. Individuals and their families always have the option to request additional testing and services which they accept personal financial responsibility for.

It should be noted; hospitalization is generally discouraged once a patient enters hospice care. While the Medicare benefit does contain provisions for short-term hospital stays (referred to as "impatient care") for symptom management, the criteria for admission and coverage for treatments are not always clear or easily defined.

Participation in experimental treatments or clinical trials are not allowed, because they are considered life-prolonging; See the topic "Understanding the difference between palliative and hospice care." In addition, other treatments or procedures considered life-prolonging are often denied. (It should be noted however, if the patient or family is willing to accept personal financial responsibility for denied requests, they will often be granted.)

Now for a word about insurance; Insurance may not fully cover hospice care for everyone. To be sure, most patients are eligible for 100% hospice coverage under Medicare called "The Hospice care benefit." There are some exceptions though. For example, if a patient goes directly to the hospital without arranging with their hospice team, their benefits could be terminated.

Families and caregivers often find themselves feeling guilty for choosing hospice care for a loved one. It is at a time like this when caregivers should be reminded that choosing this comfort care does not mean they are giving up on the one they love. Rather, they are opting for the best care and pain management available.

There are several misconceptions about hospice care. Some believe it is only available to those who are only hours away from death. In reality, it can be accessed up to six months before a person is expected to die.

It is widely believed that once a person enters hospice care they cannot leave. In fact, this care is entirely "at will." If a patient decides they no longer wish to receive care through hospice, they are free to leave without penalty. If they should later decide to re-admit themselves to the program, re-enrollment is typically permitted so long as they are still medically eligible.

A prevailing belief among some is that this specialized care is only available to the elderly. Hospice care is available to any person of any age who has received a prognosis of six months or less to live.

UNDERSTANDING THE DIFFERENCE BETWEEN PALLIATIVE AND HOSPICE CARE

While both Palliative and Hospice care focuses on the patient's physical, emotional, and mental well-being, they do have different objectives. When someone has a health condition which cannot be cured and is life threatening, both strive to meet the patient's various needs. The difference is, when Palliative care is chosen, the patient can continue to receive treatment for their illness or try to prevent further progression of the disease, or just to keep symptoms at bay.

Doctors will recommend hospice, rather than palliative care, when aggressive treatment is no longer affecting their condition, and the patient and family want care that focuses on comfort only.

One way to begin to fully understand the hospice experience is to hear from those who have experienced it. The following are some testimonials of those who have chosen the hospice option. Please note that names, locations, and personal information have been either omitted or deleted to respect the privacy of those sharing.

"I wish to spend a moment thanking all of you for the outstanding and compassionate care your staff demonstrated during my mother's last days. As one of her daughters, I was most appreciative of the tasteful surroundings that provided my mother with a sense of peace and comfort, as your facility was so warm and inviting, rather than the drab setting of some institutional settings. The kindness shown by all your staff speaks highly of your attention to detail in recruiting the right personalities who can be both honest and understanding with both the dying and grief-stricken families. I know that it is a special calling to work in a Hospice unit, but for those of you I grew to know, you touched all our lives during those dark days. May God Bless you, and may you carry yourselves through life understanding that you truly made a difference in this world."

"My experience with the hospice professionals that cared not only for my father, but our entire family during this very difficult time was nothing short of amazing. We received frequent calls to check on how the family was doing. Every caregiver was patient and empathetic.

They were flexible and accommodating with his schedule when he was so sick and at times unresponsive. We so appreciated the professional health care from both the doctors and nurses who took such good care of Dad. A special thank you to the chaplain, Rev. Cecil Rowell, as well as the many others that visited us at my father's bedside. Your careful and tender care allowed my father to pass peacefully with dignity and love surrounding him. Thank you to each and every one of you. You are all amazing people."

"During her stay, my daughter received the highest quality of care, compassion, and comfort possible. The more than competent medical and management team were so supportive of our entire family. They never seemed to tire of our questions, many of which were asked more than once. The social workers and chaplain were helpful, compassionate, and always seemed available to us. While we miss our beautiful daughter so much, we will be forever grateful to all the hospice staff for their tender and thoughtful care. You made a very difficult time easier. Thank you."

Do not shy away from looking at all options open to competent care during difficult health decisions. They are there for people who need them.

One final thought: Once a person enters hospice, if their condition changes in a positive way, they can be discharged from hospice care. When a person is discharged from hospice care, they can once again resume life giving opportunities or even participate in clinical trials. If the time comes when hospice is needed again, a person can re-enter into the program. Please note, if this is the case, there are usually time restrictions between leaving and re-entering.

Remember, hospice is and will be a different and often unique experience for all who choose to participate. As stated earlier, hospice exists to treat the patient, not the disease. This often-overlooked opportunity for end-of-life care can be a real "game changer" for loved ones as well as care givers. Hospice is a wonderful asset for end-of-life care and can be a real help to those left behind to understand and navigate days here-to-for never encountered.

BILL'S UPDATE, JUNE 2024

I have written several thoughts about the wonders of God, and what He is still teaching me. As I close in on almost 10 years since my diagnosis of stage 4 Prostate cancer and think back, I am sure I had this disease long before it was diagnosed. I am reminded daily that I have a disease that is going to kill me. During this time, I have learned a lot about my Father in heaven, and that has been wonderful!

Early on it was really bad. The Oncologist told my wife Sharon that I was in the valley of death, and we needed to have a family meeting. I was still beyond miserable. The infusions started and Intercessory Prayer Warriors continued to pray. I got better, never good, but better. After that time, I have never had a really good day, but neither have I had a horrendous day. A good medical team and strong Intercessory prayer is a great combination.

I can say with assurance that it has not been all great or even good. I have accumulated over $1,000,000 in medical bills. (As of today, I don't owe any medical bills. PTL.) I did have many "discussions" with hospitals, insurance companies, etc. and let me tell you, that can wear you out. For anyone going through anything similar to my situation I would suggest you know the details of all your insurance coverages. This is not only wise but will also give you some peace of mind in regard to the mounting costs involved.

I might also suggest if you are considered for a clinical trial or study, jump at the chance. (Someone has already done that so we might benefit from their experience.) Yes, some of the side effects can and will be uncomfortable but go into it with prayer and you will find it is not all that bad.

I knew from day one that I would not be healed. I cannot tell you why I knew this, I just did. Over the years, as the disease has overtaken my body and my life, I have come to realize I have to continually swallow my pride and ask for help. I am doing better at this, but I have not arrived.

There are other negative things you may have to deal with. I was offered an end-of-life drug. I am taking it but wish now I had not. I am having more bad days, but I will say I am ok, but to close friends, I tell the truth.

One more item before I close. Sharon, my wife of 56 years died after years of chronic pain. I have lived alone ever since. I do all the normal stuff, fix meals, do laundry, clean house, and even work in the yard occasionally. But what I am experiencing is a life of deep loneliness! I know the Father will call me home in due time, but some days it is a very real struggle.

I have found keeping the Father, The Lord Jesus, and the Holy Spirit close is so very important. I would suggest this for anyone who might be, or one day will follow this path of difficulty of knowing you are losing your battle for continued existence here in this life.

I have now completed 33 quarterly visits, MRIs, X-rays, Pet Scans, bone scans, two hospital stays and a ton of opioid pills. With all of this in my rear-view mirror, I realize heaven has taken on a whole new meaning for me.

(You can find more on these thoughts in my teaching about heaven at the back of the book)

7 DON'T STOP LIVING WHILE YOU'RE LIVING

Bill and I had been meeting for well over a year, when he surprised me one Thursday with something completely unexpected, saying, "You know LD, God spoke to me last night and said, 'quit fussing about how long you are going to live-and just do it!'" Up to this point, we had spent most of our time talking about his upcoming journey to heaven. That surprising conversation with God spawned a new and unexpected direction for our time together.

Ever since Bill's diagnosis of cancer, he emotionally and spiritually began making plans to move from this world to the next. After taking care of all the things of seeming importance on this side (wills, money, property, etc.) he began preparing for what he believed to be a new, and exciting transition.

You will recall, spiritually Bill was ready for the transition, yet God seemed to have other plans.

A few years after his initial diagnosis, his wife of 56 years became ill, and unexpectedly passed away. Shortly after the funeral, Bill fell, breaking his sternum and fracturing several ribs. The doctor said surgery was not necessary, but the pain would be quite uncomfortable.

Bill was devastated at this turn of events in his life. All his trials and frustrations simply intensified his impatience with his own transition. He continued the chemo treatments, and went through the necessary steps toward healing, but his heart was just not there! He was ready to go home. After all, everything he really cared about, except his immediate family and a few friends, was already on the other side and he wanted to be there too.

In the midst of this, Bill was once again reminded of how Jesus was continuing to work in his life. He was enjoying daily wonders with God. Lodged in his mind were the words Jesus had spoken to him at the beginning of his cancer diagnosis, "You will not die of this cancer at this time. When you have done all the work I have for you, then I'll call you home.'" At the time, he did not completely understand all the ramifications of this. Indeed, "progressive revelation" was then and still continues to be quite relevant.

It was around this time I mentioned to him about writing a book outlining his cancer journey. As noted previously, he was somewhat reluctant to make the commitment. He was averse to the idea of people looking to him as any kind of example or someone to offer advice. Eventually he agreed, but only with the stipulation that he not be looked at as some kind of "super-hero" or bigger than life person. Which brings us back to this new and unplanned chapter of his journey.

In Thornton Wilder's play "Our Town," Emily, who has died in childbirth joins the dead souls in the town cemetery and begins to view earthly life and human beings from a new perspective. In act three, she is allowed to revisit her twelfth birthday. She makes some interesting observations.

"Do any human beings ever realize life while they live it, every day, every minute?" A few lines later she exclaims, "The living don't understand the importance of human existence."

Maybe this was the message God was relaying to Bill in that late night appointment. Unfortunately, many times we fail to recognize the importance of the days allotted to us. With all the uncertainties in our world, there is one which stands clear and without question, we will one day all cease to exist upon this earth. The days given to us will never be repeated, but maybe, just maybe they can be looked at and experienced in a here-to-for unexpected way.

While embracing the universal and shared destiny of a terminal disease, Bill invites us to look at life from a different perspective for the days we do have left. Remember the days are there, the question is what we will do with them. Bill challenges each of us with the following suggestions:

Keep expecting. Never stop looking for the good of the day. One of the unforgettable lines in the play "South Pacific" was, "You gotta have a dream, cause if you never have a dream how you ever going to have a dream come true?" Bill thinks it would be fair to say the same about expectations. To stop expecting is to relegate yourself to mediocrity. If that is the path chosen, then each moment and every day is one to be endured, and seldom if ever enjoyed. It is like turning the light off in a room just when something interesting and maybe even intriguing is about to happen.

Today, you may, like Bill, be one of those people with a diagnosed terminal disease. Your sense of despair and isolation wants to rule your life. Bill would say, this is the point where a choice can be made. Will you continue to live while you are living, or will you give up and wait for the inevitable? Bill experienced those very same feelings. In looking back at his past days and experiences, he suggests the following:

In a still quiet moment courageously ask yourself, "What would I be doing with my life if this disease had not come for a permanent visit?" While embracing all the difficulties your disease has brought with it, keep on, don't stop. There is a reason God has not taken you home yet, look for it, embrace it, and live in and through it.

This line of personal introspection poses an interesting question. It becomes even more interesting because Bill would tell you he was faced with it in a very intense and personal way. He did not invite the question, but believes God wanted him to wrestle with a possibility not necessarily of his choosing. What if God were to choose to heal, or add days, weeks, months or even years to his life? He had been planning, preparing, and even expecting to soon make his heavenly transition. He had taken care of all earthly and spiritual necessities. He indeed was ready. But what if God was not? What if He had more work for him to do? Maybe like him you are sick; yes, you hurt in places you never even knew existed. You have lost your appetite, for food as well as life, but what if God says, "Not yet?"

Bill wrestled with several responses. Confusion being chief among them. This was quickly followed by a rethinking of his current situation, and even some sparks of anger towards God!

I think Bill would say it is ok to be angry with God, at least for a time. He would also say, the one overriding thing to remember is God loves you, wants to spend eternity with you, and is not leaving you on this side of your eternal home to suffer. He has a plan and a purpose. Don't give in, don't give up! Keep living. That's leveraging expectation and living through God's plan for your life.

Bill also suggests if your eternal home is not quite ready yet, maybe you could try to do some exploring. This has been a valuable personal lesson for him. Ok, spelunking is probably off the table, and a 14-hour plane ride to the Australian Outback is not in the cards, but that does not mean some personal exploring is out. You can pick up a well written book and vicariously enjoy exploring a hidden cave. Allow your mind to "see" the rich colors of the stalagmites and stalactites. Reveal in the discovery of ancient art and paintings never before seen from the ancient world.

Find an author who has traveled exclusively the Australian Continent. Enjoy the emerald rainforests, the fragrant eucalyptus covered mountains and the golden coastlines. Explore the woodland caves with their Aboriginal art. You can do all this exploring without ever leaving your comfortable recliner. (And a side benefit is that your pain just might mellow out for a bit.)

Perhaps The Bible has always been somewhat of a mystery to you. This was another lesson Bill had learned as he continued to pursue life in the present. He suggests you might want to think about enrolling in some Old or New Testament online classes. Draw up a list of questions about God which may have always bugged you. Make an appointment with a minister or your pastor and get their perspective.

When it comes to exploring, the sky is the limit! Even though your appetite has diminished, try some new food you have always been hesitant to experiment with. Bill loves chocolate and strawberry milkshakes. He says he is now pushing the envelope and trying such things as hot fudge and peanut-butter milkshakes! Reconnect with family and friends. I am sure you have noticed that there is that tendency to back away from meaningful relationships. He says this because that was his tendency. Now, he would say, don't make it just about you! Maybe they need to reconnect with you and don't know how to break through your bubble of isolation. Break the bubble for them! Be willing to take the first step. In doing so, maybe your pain will take a back seat for a time.

Find some things to laugh about, even if it is yourself. Bill admits this was of particular difficulty for him. Then he was reminded of Proverbs 17:22 which says, "Laughter is good medicine." (Or some translations say "a joyful heart is good medicine.") Note the last part of the verse, "but a broken spirit dries up the bones." He felt like at times he was "dried up" and just existing, waiting for the next minute to expire off life's time clock. That is why now he says learn to laugh again, at the very least for a few moments each day.

You will make your transition to your new home when it has been fully furnished, and the Great Mover of the universe says, "It's time." Until then, "quit fussing about how long you are going to live, and just do it." By the way, remember, this is from a man with a diagnosed terminal disease, not someone just saying things to hopefully make you feel better; feeling better probably is not going to happen, but continuing to live while you are living can have a profound effect on the days you do have left.

I have an inkling where your mind is right now after reading this. You would like to shout at me, "You just don't understand what I am going through. You don't know about my pain, the weakness in both mind and spirit. You cannot begin to imagine how tired, so very tired I am. I just don't understand why God doesn't take me home right now!"

You know what, you're right, I don't know or fully understand what you are going through right now. I only know about my journey. I do know about the pain and weakness in body and soul though. So let me just close by saying, I also have a terminal illness that is waiting to take this only life I have ever known. Like you, my days are limited, but until I hear that trumpet call, I am going to continue to live life while I am living. I invite you on the journey with me. It is looking better all the time.

One further note: Now entering into the 9th year of my initial diagnosis I must confess my faith is stronger, my outlook for eternity brighter and my relationship With Jesus Christ richer than I could have ever imagined. I am ready and anxious to spend eternity with my Savior, but until He calls me home, I think I'll just keep on living while I am living.

UPDATED JULY, 2024

These are notes and thoughts after the Zoom meeting with Dr. Parihk on July 7th, 2024.

Results of the last Pluvicto were not good. The PSA count had jumped dramatically! When starting the Pluvicto injections my PSA was 4.5., then 5.0, next 13. followed by a count of 34, and then a 44. The results I received today revealed my PSA had jumped to 135.

The trend is very revealing as well as sobering. The cancer tumor clusters have reached around 200 and are growing. Dr. Parihk wants to be sure he has all the results before making any definitive projections. I will have another set of labs in two months. The results of those labs will be a good indicator if I should begin to utilize hospice. I am aware I have many questions and some things to take care of. One of these is to begin funeral arraignments, and all that might entail.

I am deeply concerned about how my sons and grandchildren will respond when the Father says, "Your work is done son, time to come home." I believe in an instant I will leave this earth as I know it. I will transition from a mortal carbon-based body to an intermediate spiritual body. As the apostle Paul says in I Corinthians 13:12, "For now we see in a mirror dimly, but then face to face." In a twinkling of an eye, I will see Jesus face to face! Words fail to describe my feelings, but I sincerely believe that will be more than wonderful! At the same time, I may be somewhat scared and embarrassed by the few treasures I have sent to heaven's vault, while living here on this earth.

In one breath I will see Sharon followed by seeing life, not needing any "dark glass" anymore. I will meet for the first time my children who have never seen the light of day. It just goes on and on the wonderful things I will experience for eternity!

When your doctor says to you that you may be dead in a few months, you really do see life in a whole new and different way. The reality of heaven becomes richer and more real, while the hold this earth has becomes less and less. There is a very real sense of anticipation.

8 A UNIQUE PERSPECTIVE

One of the great benefits of spending hours with someone like my friend Bill are the lessons being taught and the lessons learned. Bill has not been intentionally teaching, yet that has been what is happening. I don't believe I have spent an hour with him that I have not grown in my understanding of God, as well in the intentionally of the uniqueness of how to live life.

As a Pastor, I have lost count of the times a husband or wife have come to me saying, "She just does not make me happy any longer," "he never makes me happy anymore. I think divorce is the only answer," or "I just want to be happy."

And there is the problem; Happiness! We all want, seek, enjoy and feel we deserve happiness. After spending almost every Thursday with Bill, I now realize I have a new understanding of happiness.

First, I can assure you Bill is not happy he has cancer. He is not happy his days here on earth are numbered. He is not happy about the pain that lives with him hourly. He is not happy about not being able to go fishing or teach a class or enjoy a long walk on a pleasant evening. All that said, he is one of the most joyful people I have had the privilege of associating with.

In watching and learning from my friend, I think I have learned to give up on trying to find happiness and have never been happier. In fact, I have discovered a new and enticing avenue of life, which I am learning to pursue daily. More on this later.

The Bible for me has always been a wonderful source of

encouragement, yet there are some passages which give me pause. One of those in particular is the book of James, Chapter One. "Consider it all joy, my brethren, when you encounter various trials, knowing that the testing of your faith produces endurance."

One commentator noted that trials (temptations) have the double sense of outward trials and inner temptations. In all honesty, that is right down at the bottom of my wish list! But it did send me on a quest for understanding the position of happiness verses joy.

Happiness is often elusive and difficult to find, especially when you feel you need it the most. This often causes one to go looking for it in all the wrong places, which usually causes problems instead of discovery.

It has been said that happiness is seeking pleasure and comfort. If we are to accept that as a definition, then it seems it will lead to the logical conclusion of repeated failure.

I have begun to believe happiness finds you, and not the other way around. If happiness is the goal, then disappointment will often be the result, thus my personal decision to stop pursuing happiness, and instead look and pursue joyfulness. Which brings us to what I am experiencing in a new journey of joy and happiness.

My newfound definition of joy is appreciation. Appreciation for the little things like the smell of a rose, the feel of a warm breeze on a cool day, the blue of the sky, and the awesomeness of a thunderstorm. In fact, the beauty of all God's creation!

I am beginning to see things a little differently now. When I think about life on a daily basis, things like the smile of a friend, the hug of a child, or the encouraging word that comes just when needed, I am trying to pause and drink it in through appreciation. And in finding appreciation, happiness often finds me.

I am discovering this kind of appreciation can be cultivated, practiced, and embedded into every aspect of my life. I am discovering this joy is more of an attainment than an event. It puts new perspective on how I approach my thoughts, feelings and even my actions. It is growing into a response to what really matters most in my life. That is why I can say I have given up on trying to find happiness and have never been happier.

I am finding that when appreciation is my goal, things which happen to me take on a different hue. Instead of decrying the absence of happiness, I am now magnifying the resources at my disposal when difficult things occur in my life. Instead of looking for pleasure, I am learning to look for purpose. I am learning to ask myself, what can I learn from these situations which visit without an invitation? How can I become better for the experience and not become bitter? What do I want my life to look like on the back side of difficulty, where only shame or wholeness are the choices? How do I want my children, grandchildren, and friends to remember me?

Because of my newfound discovery of appreciation, I have also been faced with the inevitable question, what if the situation does not change? How am I going to live with disability, the lack of resources, the unfairness of others actions toward me? Looking back on my life, I believe God gave me the answer to this perplexing question a number of years ago, without me fully realizing its importance. The answer was "accept and adapt." At the time it meant to accept the reality of what was happening and move past dead end emotions which were only leading to more dead ends.

I now fully realize I can appreciate the opportunity to adapt. It in no way means I like the unbidden difficulty, but rather when I accept my new reality, I can then begin to constructively deal with it. I have begun to appreciate what difficulties can do for the "inner me," and that changes everything!

I am reminded of a young man in the Bible by the name of Joseph. He was the favored son of his father and thus tended to lord his status over his brothers. One day, while away from home, his brothers decided they had enough of his self-righteousness. They took the new coat his father had just given him, stripped it from him and threw him in a pit to die. About that time, they saw a traveling caravan and decided instead of killing him they would make some money and sell him into slavery to the passing caravan. After pocketing the money from his sale, they sprinkled some lambs blood on Joseph's new coat and returned and told their father he had been killed by a wild beast.

I think we can assume this is not a situation in which Joseph found any sense of happiness. But that is only the beginning of the story and not the ending. Joseph knew the secret of accepting and adapting.

In Genesis 39, beginning with verse one we read, "Now Joseph was taken down to Egypt; and Potiphar, an Egyptian officer of Pharaoh, the captain of the bodyguard, bought him from the Ishmaelites. And the Lord was with Joseph, so he became a successful man."

Suffice to say Joseph was not happy to be taken from his home, sold into slavery and used as a servant. But he accepted and adapted to his new reality. The story continues that eventually he was put in charge of all his master owned.

He is now in a good place again in life. The problem was his master's wife was attracted to him and attempted to seduce him. When he refused her advances, she told her husband he had tried to seduce her! Of course this made his master angry on many fronts, and he had Joseph thrown into prison.

In prison, Joseph found favor with the chief jailer. Eventually he was running the prison. (He was accepting and adapting.) While in prison, he made friends with some prisoners of royalty. Eventually, two of these were released from prison and returned to the Royal service.

As so often happens with those who choose to pursue purpose and joy and not look for or expect happiness, good things happen. Such was the case in Joseph's life. It seems the King had a dream which none of his magicians or wise men could interpret. One of the released prisoners whom Joseph had befriended in prison got word to the King that Joseph had interpreted several dreams for some prisoners.

Joseph was called to the palace and asked if he could interpret the

Kings dream. Through a process of events, he did just that.

Let's pick up the story as found in Genesis chapter 41. "Then Pharaoh said to his servants, can we find a man like this, in whom is a divine spirit? So, Pharaoh said to Joseph, 'Since God has informed you of all this, there is no one so discerning and wise as you are. You shall be over my house and according to your command all my people do homage; only in the throne will I be greater than you.' And Pharaoh said to Joseph, 'I have set you over all the land of Egypt.' Then Pharaoh took off his signet ring from his hand and put it on Joseph's hand, and clothed him in fine linen, and put the gold necklace around his neck. And he set him over all the land of Egypt."

Now folks, there is a lot more to this story which I have not gone into detail about. I would suggest you read it in its entirety for context. Here is the point I would like to make: Joseph was not happy when he was thrown into a pit by his brothers. He was not happy about being sold into slavery. He was not happy being lied about by his master's wife, and he certainly was not happy about getting thrown into prison. If happiness had been his goal, he would have been an abject failure. But he accepted and adapted!

Maybe you're the one who has cancer, lost a job or loved one, been unfairly treated or even lied about. Maybe you are finding your spouse is not making you happy, or your job looks like a dead end, or your kids are doing all the wrong things.

If you find yourself in any of these types of situations, you would probably have the same problem with James in chapter one of his letters to the church in Jerusalem of which I wrestled. When bad news, difficult situations, life altering realities, and frustration abounds, joy is just not on your list of life pursuits!

So, what do you do? Accept and Adapt! This is what Bill has done, and I believe he would tell you happiness has come and blessed him countless times! He still is not happy about his health situation, or the hourly pain and sleepless nights he is enduring. But I believe he would also tell you he has found a new and deeper relationship with His Lord and Savior Jesus Christ! This from a man who already had a close relationship with Him!

Bill took advantage of the opportunities of maximizing his God given resources. Daily he acknowledges he has cancer, while he continues to learn and appreciate all God has done and is doing in his life.

He accepted and adapted to his new reality. Because of this, if you had the privilege of visiting with Bill Norris, I believe you would find a joyful man. (He might even be happy to see you!)

9 BILL'S TEACHINGS ABOUT HEAVEN

Introduction:
Discovering Session One: What do we know about heaven?
Discovering Session Two: The Present Heaven
Discovering Session Three: The New Earth
Discovering Session Four: Reigning and Ruling
Discovering Session Five: Glimpses into Heaven
Discovering Session Six: Relationships in Heaven
Discovering Session Seven: Our Greatest Adventure

INTRODUCTION TO OUR STUDY ABOUT HEAVEN

Let's make sure we are on the same page in our discussion about heaven. There is a very real "Intermediate heaven," and it exists in all of its splendor right now. Jesus, and our loved ones, are there. (We will cover that in more detail in a later lesson.) The idea of an Intermediate and a New Eternal Heaven will form the backdrop and direction for our discussions.

Our study will cover seven lessons. 1) What We Know About Heaven. 2) The Present Heaven. 3) The New Earth. 4) Reigning And Ruling. 5) Glimpses Into Heaven. 6) Relationships In Heaven. 7) Our Greatest Adventure.

Let's get started!

Discovery #1
WHAT DO WE KNOW ABOUT HEAVEN

As mentioned in our introduction, this study about heaven will focus on the now, the intermediate, and the eternal Heaven.

Discovery #1 will look at what for some may be a new perspective about our eternal dwelling place. To get started, let's read Revelation 21:1-5 (We will be using the NASB translation)

"And I saw a new heaven and a new earth; for the first heaven and the first earth passed away, and there is no longer any sea. 2) And I saw the holy city, new Jerusalem, coming down out of heaven from God, made ready as a bride adorned for her husband. 3) And I heard a loud voice from the throne saying, Behold the tabernacle of God is among men, and He shall dwell among them, and they shall be His people, and God Himself shall be among them, 4) And He shall wipe away every tear from their eyes; and there shall no longer be any death; there shall no longer be any mourning, or crying or pain; the first things have passed away. 5) And He who sits on the throne said, Behold, I am making all things new. And He said Write, for these things are faithful and true."

Notice how many times you see the word "new" and what it is referencing. It is used four times to describe heaven, earth, Jerusalem, and don't miss the word "everything." It would be difficult to miss the fact of a new world order being ushered in. This concept of a new heaven and a new earth is not confined to the New Testament alone. In Isaiah 65:17 we find the words, "For behold, I create new heavens and a new earth, And the former things shall not be remembered or come to mind. The 'New Jerusalem' takes the place of the old 'Babylon.'"

Now, let's read Revelation 21:2-3 once again. It is here we encounter one of the biggest misconceptions that the current heaven or Paradise is our final destination when we die. It seems almost second nature for us to picture the temporary or intermediate rather than the permanent. Think for a moment how the dwelling place described in Revelation 21:2-3 differs from most people's understanding of heaven. It is easy to focus on the wonderful temporary heaven, missing the opportunity to discover God's ultimate New Heaven and New Earth.

The apostle Paul's writings were big regarding heaven. As you note Philippians 3:13-14 and Colossians 3:1-2 you will find a calm sense of serenity and expectation. Philippians 3:13-14 reads, "13) Brethren, I do not regard myself as having laid hold of it yet, but one thing I do: forgetting what lies behind and reaching forward to what lies ahead, 14) I press on toward the goal for the prize of the upward call of God In Christ Jesus." Colossians 3:1-2 reads, "If you have been raised up with Christ, keep seeking the things above, where Christ is seated at the right hand of God. 2) Set your mind on the things above, not on the things that are on the earth."

King David reveals how he saw heaven in Psalms 27:4, "One thing I have asked from the Lord, that shall I seek: That I may dwell in the house of the lord all the days of my life. To behold the beauty of the Lord, And to meditate in His temple." And again, in Psalms 42:1-2, "As the deer pants for the water brooks, so my soul pants for Thee, O God. My soul thirsts for God, for the living God. When shall I come and appear before God?"

David seems to be emitting an excited goal or prize, much like Paul. One erroneous view of heaven is a concept called "Christo Platonism." It has been around since the time of the Greek philosopher Plato. He wrongly taught that the body is material and everything else is spirit. Therefore, heaven, if it even exists, cannot be physical and is only a place of disembodied spirits. I trust we can all agree that Plato was 100% wrong! Generally, today, when people think about heaven it is usually in the form of the things they are going to enjoy and give little thought about Jesus.

Heaven is not an eternal church service. People do not become angels. People are not some ethereal disembodied entities. There is no such thing as soul sleep. The list could go on and on about what some think heaven is, when in reality they often miss the more important Biblical view. Heaven is a real place with real people in real relationships. In fact, it most probably is more real than we can even imagine. What we do receive in heaven is precisely what Jesus promises: a resurrected life, in a resurrected body, with a resurrected Jesus living on a resurrected earth.

In Isaiah 65: 17-25, we find what appears to be a double vision, or one overlapping the other. One is a vision of the New Earth and another of the Millennium. As you read, be careful to not mix them up. This will only cause you confusion. Isaiah 65:17-19 talks about the New Earth. Verses 20-24 deal with the Millennium. Verse 25 references a time in the New Earth when man and wild animals will coexist in total harmony. As you read these verses, allow them to give assurance to your heart that you will one day live in a perfect world with Almighty God and His Son Jesus for eternity.

"For behold, I create new heavens and a new earth, and the former things will not be remembered or come to mind. 18) But be glad and rejoice forever in what I create; For behold I create Jerusalem for rejoicing, and her people for gladness. 19) I will also rejoice in Jerusalem and be glad in my people, And there will no longer be heard in her the voice of weeping and the sound of crying. 20) No longer will there be in it an infant who lives but a few days, Or an old man who does not live out his days. For the youth will die at the age of one hundred, And the one who does not reach the age of one hundred shall be thought accursed. 21) And they shall build houses and inhabit them; They shall also plant vineyards and eat their fruit. 22) They shall not build and another inhabit, they shall not plant and another eat; For as the lifetime of a tree, so shall be the days of My people, And My chosen ones shall wear out the work of their hands. 23) They shall not labor in vain, Or build children for calamity; For they are the offspring of those blessed by the Lord, and their descendants with them. 24) It will also come to pass that before they call, I will answer; and while they are still speaking, I will hear. 25) The wolf and the lamb shall graze together, and the lion shall eat straw like the ox, and dust shall be the serpent's food. They shall do no evil or harm in all My holy mountain, says the Lord."

John is given a revelation of life on the new earth, found in Revelation 22:1-6. We can only imagine what it will be like, but it was

God who gave us an imagination, so let's imagine! Can you begin to picture what it will be like to live in a clean, beautiful, and perfect world? I can only imagine. Sounds like a good title for a song (oops, I think it has already been created)!

"And he showed me a river of the water of life, clear as crystal, coming from the throne of God and of the Lamb. 2) In the middle of its street. And on either side of the river was the tree of life, bearing twelve kinds of fruit, yielding its fruit every month: And the leaves of the tree were for the healing of the nations. 3) And there shall no longer be any curse, and the throne of God and of the Lamb shall be in it and His bond servants shall serve Him. 4) And they shall see His face and their and His name shall be on their foreheads. 5) And there shall no longer be any night; and they shall not have need of the light of the lamp, nor the light of the sun because the Lord God shall illumine them; and they shall reign forever and ever. 6) And He said to me, these words are faithful and true, and the Lord, the God of the spirits of the prophets, sent his angel to show to His bond servants the things which must shortly take place." Revelation 22:1-6.

Job of the Old Testament is often considered a gloomy Gus but listen to his words as he deals with tragedy after tragedy. "And as for me, I know that my Redeemer lives, and at the last He shall take His stand on the earth 26) Even after my skin is destroyed, yet from my flesh I shall see God. Whom I myself shall behold, and whom my eyes shall see and not another." Job19; 25-27.

Even in his darkest days, when everything earthly has been taken from him, and family and friends have forsaken, he still presents a settled assurance in his extreme trials.

David declares in Psalm 27:4, "One thing I have asked from the Lord, that shall I seek; that I may dwell in the house of the Lord all the days of my life, to behold the beauty of the Lord, and to meditate in His temple." Think about it; to be with Jesus in heaven forever, where He rules and reigns, then we have unbroken fellowship with Him. Oh, how I want to know and one day see Jesus; yet greater still, how I long for Jesus to know me, and look upon me with acceptance and love.

We understand our ultimate destination will not be reached on this side of heaven. Revelation 21:2-3 reminds us that when that day comes, God will live with us. Praise His Name!

Discovery #2
THE PRESENT HEAVEN

This session will cover some thoughts and clarifications about who is now physically in heaven. Let's first begin with the answer and then show you the biblical background for our conclusions. Who is in heaven "right now?" Answer: All of our loved ones and all those who have passed on knowing Jesus Christ as their personal savior. This would of course include such biblical personalities such as Moses, Elijah, Enoch, Lazarus, the thief on the cross, the apostle Paul, 500 witnesses after the first Easter, Martyred saints, all of the Hebrew references, and most importantly, Jesus after His Ascension. (This is only a portion of those enjoying the wonders of heaven. Space does not allow for a full list or accounting.)

Now, for some scriptural background for these statements:
JESUS:
"And after He had said these things, He was lifted up while they were looking on, and a cloud received Him out of their sight. And as they were gazing intently into the sky while He was departing, behold two men in white clothing stood beside them; and they also said, men of Galilee, why do you stand looking into the sky? This Jesus, who has been taken from you into heaven, will come in just the same way as you have watched Him go into heaven." (Acts 1:9-11).

Context:
Jesus has just given the Great Commission, described how they would receive the power to carry out this commission, and how they were to be His witnesses throughout the world. Angels appeared and assured them that Jesus had been taken up into heaven and would

one day return from heaven. This is the foundation for the reality of the Second Coming of Jesus.

The Criminal On The Cross:
"And one of the criminals who were hanged there was hurling abuse at Him, saying, 'Are you not the Christ? Save Yourself and us!' But the other answered and rebuking him said, 'Do you not even fear God, since you are under the same sentence of condemnation? And we indeed justly, for we are receiving what we deserve for our deeds; but his man has done nothing wrong.' And he was saying, 'Jesus, remember me when You come into Your kingdom!' And He said to him, 'Truly I say to you, today you shall be with Me in Paradise.'" (Luke 23:39-43).

Context:
Jesus has received his death sentence from the gathered Jews. Simon bears Jesus' cross followed by a great multitude to the place of execution. He is hung on a cross between two criminals. One criminal hurls insults and taunts Jesus. One rebukes his fellow criminal and asks Jesus to remember him when He comes into His Kingdom. Jesus assures the penitent criminal that this very day he would be with Him in Paradise.

The word "Paradise" came originally from Persia and denoted a beautiful pleasure garden. It came to mean a place of happiness, and here it refers to heaven.

Paul:
"Boasting is necessary, though it is not profitable; but I will go on to visions and revelations of the Lord. I know a man in Christ who fourteen years ago, weather in the body, I do not know, or out of the body I do not know, God knows, such a man was caught up to the third heaven. And I know how such a man, weather in the body or apart from the body I do not know, God knows, was caught up into Paradise and heard inexpressible words, which a man is not permitted to speak." (II Corinthians 12: 1-4).

Context:
Paul was granted a moment of intimate companionship with Jesus within the courts of heaven itself. How wonderful was the experience? He did not know if he was in or out of the body. This is the second of only three uses of the word "Paradise." The first we have already highlighted in the recounting of the thief on the cross. The third reference can be found in Revelation 2:7, "He who has an ear, let him hear what the Spirit says to the churches, To him who overcomes I will grant to eat of the tree of life, which is in the Paradise of God."

The verb used is the same in all three instances, but here in 11 Corinthians it is now used to describe the third heaven.

While I do not agree with all of William Barclay's theological concepts, he does present a beautiful description of this word Paradise. (You will recall from an earlier description of the term Paradise; it denoted a beautiful pleasure garden.) "When a Persian king wished to confer a very special honor on someone who was especially dear to him, he made him a companion of the garden and gave him the right to walk in the royal gardens with him in close and intimate companionship."

There does not seem to be any theological reason to distinguish between the meanings of the three New Testament occurrences of Paradise.

500 Witnesses:
"For I delivered to you as of first importance what I also received, that Christ died for our sins according to the Scriptures, and that He was buried, and that He was raised on the third day according to the scriptures, and that he appeared to Cephas, then to the twelve. After that he appeared to more than five hundred brethren at one time, most of whom remain now, but some have fallen asleep; then He appeared to James, then to all the apostles; and last of all, as it were to the one untimely born, He appeared to me also." (1Corinthians 15:3-8).

Context:
Paul is addressing those who "actually" saw the risen Christ. In the list we find Peter (Cephas), The Twelve (actually there were only 10 at Jesus first appearance to them, Judas having committed suicide and Thomas being absent).

"The Twelve" is often used in scripture to identify the original apostles. Then over five hundred witnesses, Next, He appears to James, and last (Paul identifies as least) Resurrected Jesus appears to Paul. Quite a list of esteemed individuals.

Martyred Tribulation Saints:
"And when He broke the fifth seal, I saw underneath the altar the souls of those who had been slain because of the testimony which they had maintained; and they cried out with a loud voice, saying, 'How long O Lord, holy and true, wilt Thou reframe from judging and avenging our blood on those who dwell on the earth?' And there was given to each of them a white robe; and they were told that they should rest for a little while longer, until the number of their fellow servants and their brethren who were to be killed even as they had been, should be completed also." (Revelation 6:9-11).

Context:
Note they have voices, bodies to hold robes, they can rest and talk with one another.

Stephen:
"Now when they heard this, they were cut to the quick, and they began gnashing their teeth at him. But being filled with the Holy Spirit, he gazed intently into heaven and saw the glory of God, and Jesus standing at the right hand of God." (Acts 7:54-56).

Context:
Stephen, the first Christian Martyr, amid losing his earthly life, looks and sees God and Jesus in Heaven.

Enoch:
"And Enoch lived sixty-five years and became the father of Methuselah. Then Enoch walked with God three hundred years after he became the father of Methuselah, and he had other sons and daughters. So, all the days of Enoch were three hundred and sixty-five years. And Enoch walked with God; and he was not, for God took him." (Genesis 5:23-24).

"By faith Enoch was taken up so he should not see death; and he was not found because God took him up; for he obtained the witness that before his being taken up he was pleasing to God."

Context:
There is a split focus in these passages. One walking in obedience and being pleasing to God, close fellowship, and of course faith. We might want to add, do not miss the wording "he was taken up."

Elijah:
"And then it came about as they were going along and talking, that behold there appeared a chariot of fire and horses of fire which separated the two of them and Elijah went up by a whirlwind to heaven." (11 Kings 2:11-12).

Context:
    Another steadfast and obedient servant is "seen" going up into heaven.

Rich Man and Lazarus:
"And there was a certain rich man, and he habitually dressed in purple and fine linen, gaily living in splendor every day. And a certain poor man named Lazarus was laid at his gate covered in sores, and longing to be fed with the crumbs which were falling from the rich man's table; besides, even the dogs were coming and licking his sores. Now it came to pass that the poor man died and he was carried away by the angels to Abraham's bosom; and the rich man died and was buried. And in Hades he lifted up his eyes, being in torment, and saw Abraham far away and Lazarus in his bosom. And he cried out and said, Father Abraham, have mercy on me, and send Lazarus that

he may dip the tip of his finger in water and cool off my tongue; for I am in agony in this flame. But Abraham said, 'Child remember that during your life you received your good things, and likewise Lazarus bad things; but now he is being comforted here and you are in agony. And beside all this, between us and you there is a great chasm fixed, in order for those who wish to come over from here to you may not be able, and that none may cross over from there to us.' And he said, 'Then I beg you, Father, that you send him to my father's house-for I have five brothers, that he may warn them, lest they also come to this place of torment.' But Abraham said, 'They have Moses and the prophets; let them hear them.' But he said, 'No Father Abraham, but if someone goes to them from the dead, they will repent!' But he said to him, 'If they do not listen to Moses and the Prophets, neither will they be persuaded if someone rises from the dead.'"

Context:
You will notice this is the only illustration or event that Jesus uses the proper name of a person. Also note, Lazarus has a body. He can dip his physical finger in a physical water receptacle. The rich man has a tongue, can feel pain, has emotional regrets, and even shows great love for his family.

WHO ELSE WILL BE THERE?

Ourselves, as well as all Christians who have gone before us. (As noted previously, the term "Christian" is used to describe those who have acknowledged their personal sin, taken responsibility for such, repented of their sins and established a personal relationship with Jesus Christ.)

"For we know that when this earthly tent we live in is taken down (that is when we die and leave this earthly body), we will have a house in heaven, eternal body made for us by God Himself and not by human hands. (2) for we grow weary in our present bodies, and we long to put on our heavenly bodies like new clothing. (3) For we will put on heavenly bodies; we will not be spirits without bodies. (4) While we live in these earthly bodies, we groan and sigh, but it's not that we want to die and get rid of these bodies that clothe us. Rather, we want to put on our new bodies so that these dying bodies will be swallowed up by life. (5) God Himself has prepared us for this, and as a guarantee He has given us His Holy Spirit."

SOME RESEARCH NOTES ON 2 CORINTHIANS 5:2-3

Paul changes his metaphor slightly. God will "clothe" us with a new and better garment. This new covering (dwelling from heaven) apparently awaits us immediately after death and before our resurrection. Paul clarified that believers who die are not disembodied spirits ("found naked") until the resurrection of their bodies.

I believe one of the strongest arguments that we will never be disembodied spirits is that the Bible consistently views humans as unified beings. It does not describe the body as merely the house that the real person lives in. That is a Platonic concept that the early Gnostics held. Rather, the Bible describes people as consisting of both material and immaterial parts. If we were to lack material substance (either mortal or immortal) we would seemingly be less than complete human beings.

Even though there is no specific instruction in scripture that I could find concerning an "intermediate body" and its characteristics, its existence seems beyond reasonable doubt. References to believers-- after death and before the resurrection - suggest that they have bodies. (cf. Lazarus, Luke 16:19-25; Moses and Elijah on the Mount of Transfiguration, Matthew 17:1-3 (the martyred dead in heaven).

2 Corinthians 5:6-8 says, "So we are always confident, even though we know that as long as we live in these bodies we are not at home with the Lord. (7) For we live by believing and not by seeing. Yes, we are fully confident, I say, and willing rather to be absent from the body and present with the Lord."

Compare 2 Corinthians 5:1-3 with Philippians 3:20-21. Our

immediate body and our resurrected body are NOT the same. (Agree or disagree?)

Note: The intermediate body is not the resurrected body. We will get that either at the beginning or end of the millennium.

2 Corinthians 5:1
"For we know that when this earthly tent we live in is taken down (that is when we die and leave this earthly body), we will have a house in heaven, an eternal made for us by God Himself and not by human hands. (2) we grow weary in our present bodies, and we long to put on our heavenly bodies like new clothing. (3) FOR WE WILL PUT ON HEAVENLY BODIES; WE WILL NOT BE SPIRITS WITHOUT BODIES!"

Philippians 3:20-21
"But we are citizens of heaven, where the Lord Jesus Christ lives. And we are eagerly waiting for him to return as our Savior. (21) He will take our weak mortal bodies and change them into glorious bodies like his own, using the same power with which He will bring everything under His control."

WE LIVE IN A NEW EARTH THAT HAS NOT BEEN CREATED. SO WHAT IS THE ALTERNATIVE?

ANSWER:
An intermediate Heaven that is very real and very wonderful. Some differentiate and call it Paradise.

WHAT IS THE INTERMEDIATE HEAVEN?

Answer:
God's tabernacle, angels, God's throne, and Jesus.

Just a thought, not backed up with scripture; I wonder if Jesus is constructing a 1,500-mile cube city, and if we will see it being built
Hebrews 8:5, "They serve in a system of worship that is only a copy, a shadow of the real one in heaven. For when Moses was getting

ready to build the Tabernacle, God gave him a warning: 'Be sure that you make everything according to the pattern I have given you here on the mountain.;"

Hebrews 9:11
"So Christ has now become the High Priest over all the good things that have come. He has entered that greater, more perfect Tabernacle in heaven, which was not made by human hands and is not part of this created world.

Hebrews 9:24
"For Christ did not enter into a holy place made with human hands which was only a copy of the true one in heaven. HE ENTERED INTO HEAVEN ITSELF to appear now before God on our behalf."

Hebrews 12:22
"No you have come to Mount Zion, to the city of the living God, the heavenly Jerusalem, and to countless thousands of angels in a joyful gathering."

DO WE HAVE ANY IDEA WHAT THE INTERMEDIATE HEAVEN WILL LOOK LIKE?

Personal opinion: A little bit like the Tabernacle of the Old Testament, only far more magnificent.

Hebrews 9:24
"For Christ did not enter into a holy place made with human hands, which was only a copy of the true one in heaven. He entered into heaven itself to appear now before God on our behalf."

Is there a current Tabernacle or Holy place? Is it real with a real and physical Jesus?

Isaiah 6:1-4
"It was in the year that King Uzzah died that I saw the Lord. He was sitting on a lofty throne, and the train of His robe filled the Temple.

Attending Him were mighty seraphim, each having six wings. With two wings they covered their faces, with two they covered their feet, and with two they flew. They were calling out to each other, 'Holy, Holy, Holy, is the Lord of Heaven's Armies! The whole earth is filled with His glory!' Their voices shook the Temple to its foundations, and the entire building was filled with smoke."

Revelation 4: 1-8
"Then as I looked, I saw a door standing open in heaven, and the same voice I had heard before spoke to me like a trumpet blast. The voice said, 'Come up here and I will show you what must happen after this.' And instantly I was in the Spirit, and I saw a throne in heaven and someone sitting on it. The one sitting on the throne was as brilliant as gemstones-like jasper and carnelian. And the glow of an emerald circled His throne like a rainbow. Twenty-four thrones surrounded Him-and twenty-four elders sat on them. They were all clothed in white and had gold crowns on their heads. From the Throne came flashes of lightening and the rumble of thunder. And in front of the Throne were seven torches with burning flames. This is the sevenfold Spirit of God. In the front of the Throne was a shiny sea of glass, sparkling like crystal. In thew center and around the Throne were four living beings, each covered with eyes front and back. The first of these living beings was like a lion; the second was like an ox, the third had a human face; and the fourth was like an eagle in flight. Each of these living beings had six wings, and their wings were covered all over with eyes, inside and out. Day after day and night after night they keep on saying, 'Holy, Holy, Holy is the Lord God, the Almighty, the One who was, who is, and who is still to come.'"

Acts 7:55
"But Stephen, full of the Holy Spirit, gazed steadily into heaven and saw the glory of God, and he saw Jesus standing in the place of honor at God's right hand. And he told them, 'Look I see the heavens opened and the Son of Man standing in the place of honor at God's right hand.'"

What about any construction projects going on in the intermediate heaven?

(See Revelation 21:2-3 and John 14: 1-4)
 The New Jerusalem presently being built in heaven. The saved reside there now. 1,500 miles cubed. A city this size starting in the middle of the United States would stretch from Canada to Mexico and from the Appalachian Mountains to the California border. (Randy Alcorn, Jerusalem's dimensions, February 22, 2010.)

12 gates comes to new earth after the millennium will last forever.

Gates to New Heavens

 The new Jerusalem that will come to the New Earth when it and the New Heavens are created at the end of the millennium

Revelation 21: 2-3
 "And I saw the Holy City, the New Jerusalem, coming down from God out of heaven like a bride beautifully dressed for her husband. I heard a loud shout from the Throne saying, 'Look, God's home is now among His people! He will live with them, and they will be His people. God Himself will be with them.'"

John 14:1-4
 "Do not let your hearts be troubled. Trust in God; trust also in Me. In My Father's house are many rooms; if it were not so, I would have told you. I am going there to prepare a place for you, I will come back and take you to be with Me, that you also may be where I am. You know the way to the place where I am going."

WHAT HAPPENS IN LUKE 15: 3-10?
 What does that say about those who are now in heaven? Look closely. Who does the rejoicing? What does that say about our loved ones who are now in heaven? Just something for you to think about.

I think a possible answer might be that there is rejoicing over repentant sinners. God rejoices, the angels rejoice and perhaps the great cloud of witnesses we see in Hebrews. This will not happen in the New Earth, because there is no sin.

Luke 15:3-10
"So Jesus told them this story: 'If a man has a hundred sheep and one of them gets lost, what will he do? Won't he leave the ninety-nine in the wilderness and go to search for the one that is lost until he finds it? And when he has found it he will joyfully carry it home on his shoulders. When he arrives, he will joyfully call his friends and neighbors together, saying, rejoice with me because I have found my lost sheep. In the same way, there is more joy in heaven over one lost sinner who repents and returns to God than over ninety-nine others who are righteous and haven't strayed away! Or suppose a woman has ten silver coins and loses one. Won't she light a lamp and sweep the entire house and search carefully until see finds it? And when she finds it, she will call her friends and neighbors and say, rejoice with me because I have found my lost coin. In the same way, there is joy in the presence of God and angels when even one sinner repents."

WHEN WILL THE RESURRECTION OCCUR AND WHAT MAY OCCUR BEFORE THIS HAPPENS?

This is a bit unclear to me, but I would suggest that it occurs at the Rapture, or at the end of the Millennium.

I Corinthians 15:21-24
"So, you see, just as death came into the world through a man, now the resurrection of the dead has begun through another man. Just as everyone dies because we all belong to Adam, everyone who belongs to Christ will be given a new life. But there is an order to this resurrection: Christ was raised as the first of the harvest; then all who belong to Christ will be raised when He comes back. After that the end will come, when He will turn the Kingdom over to God the Father, having destroyed every ruler and authority and power."

Discovery #3
THE NEW EARTH

Philippians 3:20-21
"But we are citizens of heaven, where the Lord Jesus Christ lives. And we are eagerly waiting for Him to return as our Savior. He will take our weak mortal bodies and change them into glorious bodies like His own, using the same power with which He will bring everything under His control."

WHY IS JESUS RESURRECTION SO IMPORTANT?
It is the reason for creation and our eternal future.

1 Corinthians 15:12-20
"But tell me this- since we preach Christ rose from the dead, why are some of you saying there will be no resurrection of the dead? For if there is no resurrection from the dead, then Christ has not been raised either. And if Christ has not been raised, then all our preaching is useless, and your faith is useless And we apostles would all be lying about God-for we have said that God raised Christ from the grave. But that can't be true if there is no resurrection from the dead. And if there is no resurrection from the dead then Christ has not been raised. And if Christ has not been raised, then your faith is useless and you are still guilty of your sins. In that case, all who died believing in Christ are lost! And if our hope in Christ is only for this life, we are more to be pitied than anyone in the world. But in fact Christ has been raised form he dead. He is the first of a great harvest of all who have died.

ADAM AND EVE WERE DRIVEN FROM THE GARDEN OF EDEN. WHAT HAS HAPPENED ON EARTH SINCE THAT TERRIBLE DAY?
Easy answer: Rampant sin, sorrow, and an ever raising of evil

Genesis 3: 14-19
"Then the Lord said to the serpent, 'Because you have done this, you are cursed more than animals, domestic and wild. You will crawl on your belly, groveling in the dust as long as you live. And I will cause

hostility between you and the woman, and between your offspring and her offspring. He will strike your head, and you will strike his heel.' Then He said to the woman, 'I will sharpen the pain of your pregnancy and in pain you will give birth. And you will desire to control your husband, but he will rule over you.' And to the man He said, 'Since you listened to your wife and ate from the tree whose fruit I commanded you not to eat, the ground is cursed because of you. All your life you will struggle to scratch a living from it. It will grow thorns and thistles for you, though you will eat of its grains. But the sweat of your brow you will have food to eat until you return to the ground from which you were made. For you were made from dust, and to dust you will return.'"

HOW DOES 1CORINTHIANS 15:21-23 SOLVE THE PROBLEM OF GENESIS 3:14-19?
Because Jesus' sacrifice on the cross made us new citizens of heaven. None of these citizens ever die!

I Corinthians 15:21-23
"So you see, just as death came into the world through a man, now the resurrection from the dead has begun through another man. Just as everyone dies because we belong to Adam, everyone who belongs to Christ will be given new life. But here is an order to this resurrection: Christ was raised as the first of the harvest; then all who belong to Christ will be raised when He comes back."

LOOK CLOSELY AT MATTHEW 19:28-29. WHAT VITALLY IMPORTANT TRUTH IS JESUS TEACHING?
He is coming back when the whole world is made new!

"And Jesus said to them, 'Truly I say you, that you who have followed Me, in the regeneration when the Son of Man will sit on His glorious throne, you also shall sit upon twelve thrones, judging the twelve tribes of Israel. And everyone who has left houses or brothers or sisters or father or mother or children or farms for My name's sake, shall receive many times as much, and shall inherit eternal life.'"

TAKE A MOMENT AND REFLECT ON ISAIAH 60:5, 11 AND 15. WHAT EMOTIONS DOES ISAIAH'S WRITINGS EVOKE?
The answer is Utter Tranquility!

Isaiah 60:5 "Then you will look and be radiant, your heart will throb and swell with joy."

Isaiah 60:11 "Your gates will always stand open, they will never be shut, day or night."

Isaiah 60:15 "Although you have been forsaken and hated, with no one traveling through, I will make you the everlasting pride and the joy of all generations."

THE CURSE WILL FOREVER BE LIFTED. WHAT DOES THAT MEAN TO YOU?
The obvious answer and good news is No More Sin!

Revelation 22:3 "No longer will there be a curse on anything. For the throne of God and of the Lamb will be there, and His servants will worship Him."

Isaiah 65:17 "Look! I am creating new heavens and a new earth, and no one will even think about the old ones anymore."

IN 1 CORINTHIANS 15:53 PAUL TALKS ABOUT IMMORTALITY. WHAT DOES IMMORTALITY MEAN TO YOU? AS YOU THINK ABOUT OUR BODIES BEING MADE IMPERISHABLE, WHAT DO YOU CONSIDER TO BE THE MOST EXCITING THING THAT YOU LOOK FORWARD TO PERSONALLY EXPERIENCING?

Most would say perfect health! No hearing aids, no drugs, no cancer, and you will even be able to leap tall buildings in a single bound!

I Corinthians 15:53 "For our dying bodies must be transformed into bodies that will never die; our mortal bodies must be transformed into immortal bodies.

Revelation 21:3-6 "I heard a loud voice from the throne saying, 'Look, God's throne is now among His people! He will live with them, and they will be His people. God Himself will be with them. He will wipe away every tear from their eyes, and there will be no more death or sorrow or crying or pain. All these things are gone forever.' And the one sitting on the throne said, 'Look I am making everything new.' and then he said to me, 'write this down, for what I said to you is trustworthy and true."

AS YOU THINK ABOUT OUR BODIES BEING MADE IMPERISHABLE, WHAT DO YOU CONSIDER TO BE THE MOST EXCITING THING WHEN IT COME TO RELATIONSHIPS?

For me it will be talking with Jesus and Christians for eternity!

AGAIN, THINK DEEPLY ABOUT PHILIPPIANS 3:20-21. THESE VERSES CONTAIN A WONDERFUL TRUTH AND PROMISE THAT IS ALMOST INCONCEIVABLE. WHAT ARE THEY? HOW DOES THAT MAKE YOU FEEL?

This is where it gets exciting! We get new bodies, changed into the glorious type of body that Jesus has! Our first body was carbon based and mortal. Our new one will be eternal! Praise God!

Philippians 3:20-21 "But we are citizens of heaven, where the Lord Jesus Christ lives. And we are eagerly waiting for Him to return as our Savior. He will take our weak mortal bodies and change them into glorious bodies like His own, using the same power with which He will bring everything under His control!"

Discovery #4
REIGNING AND RULING

THIS SECTION IS SET IN THE NEW EARTH AND THE PERMANENT HEAVEN. JESUS ALONG WITH THE REST OF THE RESIDENTS OF THE INTERMEDIATE HEAVEN, ARE RESIDING ON PLANET EARTH IN THE NEW EARTH.

God has a plan for His people. Some were great "Saints' of the Old Testament. Some are Saved Saints of the New Testament. How does this help us understand what God has planned for His children?

(Hebrews 11:39-40; 12:22-24; Isaiah 26:19)
The answer seems to be that someday we will all be made perfect in heaven with all the saints who have ever lived. We will see Jesus' face to face! Now that is worth getting excited about!

Hebrews 11:39-40" All these people earned a good reputation because of their faith, yet none of them received all that God had promised. For God had something better in mind for us, so that they would not reach perfection without us." (NLT)

Hebrews 12:22-24 "No, you have to come to Mount Zion, to the city of the living God, the heavenly Jerusalem, and to countless thousands of angels in a joyful gathering. You have come to the assembly of God's firstborn children, whose names are written in heaven. You have come to God Himself, who is the judge over all things. You have come to the spirits of the righteous ones in heaven who have now been made perfect. You have come to Jesus, the one who mediates the new covenant between God and people, and to the sprinkled blood, which speaks of forgiveness, instead of crying out for vengeance like the blood of Able."

Isaiah 26:19 "But Those who die in the Lord will live; their bodies will rise again! Those who sleep in the earth will rise up and sing for joy! For your life-giving light will fall like dew on your people in the place of the dead."

GOD MADE US FOR EARTH AND OUR FINAL DESTINATION IS THE NEW EARTH. JUST AS HE WILL MAKE US NEW IN RESURRECTED FORM, SO HE WILL MAKE THE EARTH NEW IN ITS ORIGINAL FORM. WE WILL BE ABLE TO ENJOY NATURE AS NEVER BEFORE. PEOPLE OFTEN GET CONFUSED ABOUT THE NEW EARTH. HOW WOULD YOU EXPLAIN IT TO THEM? (REVELATION 21:1-2 GIVES US SOME INSIGHT)

The indicated answer seems to be that earth as we know it will be more beautiful with breathtaking scenery being a daily occurrence. The Holy City coming down from heaven! (What an amazing reality!!)

Revelation 21:1-2 "Then I saw a new heaven and a new earth, for the first heaven and the first earth had passed away, and there was no longer any sea. I saw The Holy City, the new Jerusalem, coming down out of heaven from God, prepared a bride beautifully dressed for her husband."

LIKE PAUL, PETER HAD STRONG FEELINGS ABOUT HEAVEN. WHAT DOES HE SAY THE WORLD WOULD BE FULL OF? HOW DOES THAT IMPACT YOU ON THE EMOTIONAL LEVEL?

Peter strongly implies God's Righteousness will fill the whole world. Contrast that with the current world of sin. Without doubt, it will be wonderful beyond imagination.

2 Peter 3:13 "But we are looking forward to the new heavens and new earth he has promised, a world filled with God's righteousness."

MOSES WRITING IN THE OLD TESTAMENT LEARNED AN IMPORTANT TRUTH FROM GOD ABOUT WHAT LIFE WAS LIKE PRIOR TO THE CURSE. WHA DOES GENESIS 3: 8-10 TELL US ABOUT THE NEW EARTH WILL BE LIKE WHEN THE CURSE IS FINALLY REMOVED?

We realize we won't just see God. He will actually walk with us in a wonderful relationship.

Genesis 3:8-10 "When the cool evening breezes were blowing, the man and his wife heard the Lord God walking about in the garden. So they hid from the Lord God among the trees. Then the Lord God called to the man, 'Where are you?' He replied, 'I heard You walking in the garden, so I hid. I was afraid because I was naked.'"

IN JESUS FINAL RECORDED PRAYER, HE PRAYED "FATHER, I WANT

THOSE YOU HAVE GIVEN ME TO BE WITH ME". (AMAZING) DIGEST THAT FOR A MOMENT AND THEN LET'S DISCUSS LEVITICUS 26: 11-12 AND JOHN 17:24

(Never forget, God's love will be personal and we will be His treasured possession.)

Leviticus 26:11 "I will live among you, and I will not dispose Of you. I will walk among you; I will be your God, and you will be My people."

John 17:24 "Father, I want these You have given me to be with me where I am. Then they can see all the glory You gave me because You loved me even before the world began!"

READ REVELATION 20:6 AND 22:3-5. WE ARE TOLD AS CHRISTIANS WE WILL REIGN WITH JESUS. FIRST FOR 1000 YEARS AND THEN FOREVER AND EVER. SO WHAT IS THE DIFFERENCE?

For an answer, we have to understand the millennium starts when Jesus comes back the second time. Eternity occurs at the end of the 1000 years. Which brings us to an interesting question. What happens after the 1000-year reign? Jesus gives His kingdom to The Father. This is one of those areas I am not clear on. I invite you to think about it with me.

Revelation 20:6 "Blessed and Holy are those who share in the first resurrection. For them, the second death holds no power, but he will be priests of God and of Christ and will reign with Him a thousand years."

Revelation 22:3-5 "No longer will there be any curse upon anything. For the throne of God and of The Lamb will be there, and His servants will worship Him. And they will see His face, and His name will be written on their foreheads. And there will be no night there-no need for lamps or sun-for the Lord God will shine on them. And they shall reign forever and ever.

A personal question for you to think upon; How will you reign in the new heavens?

A possible answer could be by using our current spiritual gifts. Our bodies get a resurrected body like Jesus (Philippians 3:21). So why would spiritual gifts not do the same? Please note: This is not based on scripture but is an intriguing thought to wrestle with.

Discovery #5
GLIMPSES INTO HEAVEN

Philippians 3:20-21 "But we are citizens of heaven, where the Lord Jesus Christ lives. And we are eagerly awaiting Him to return as our Savior. He will take our weak mortal bodies and change them into glorious bodies like his own, using the same power with which He will bring everything under His control.

THE FATHER CREATED A PERFECT EARTH IN A PERFECT ENVIRONMENT. ADAM AND EVE LIVED AND ENJOYED THIS CREATION BUT WE DON'T KNOW FOR HOW LONG. THEN SIN ENTERED AND EVERYTHING CHANGED. GOD DECLARED A CURSE ON MANKIND. WHAT WAS IT?

The only answer would have to be death and a sin filled world.

Genesis 3:16-24 "Then He said to the woman, 'I will sharpen the pain of your pregnancy and in pain you will give birth. And you will desire to control your husband, but he will rule over you.' And to the man He said, 'since you listened to your wife and ate from the tree whose fruit I commanded you not to eat, the ground is cursed because of you. All your life you will struggle to scratch a living from it. It will grow thorns and thistles for you, though you eat of its grains. By the sweat of your brow, you will have food to eat until you return to the ground from which you were made. For you were made from the dust and to dust you will return.' Then the man – Adam - named his wife Eve because she would be the mother of all who live. And the Lord made clothing from animal skins for Adam and his wife. Then the Lord

God said 'look, the human beings have become like us, knowing both good and evil. What if they reach out and take fruit from the tree of life and eat it? Then they will live forever!' So, the Lord God banished them from the Garden of Eden, and He sent Adam out to cultivate the ground from which he had been made. After sending them out, the Lord God stationed mighty Cherubim to the east of the Garden of Eden. And He placed a flaming sword that flashed back and forth to guard the way to the tree of life.

WHAT PART OF CREATION SUFFERED UNDER THE CURSE?

(Romans 8:19-23)
The answer we are confronted with daily is not only all the earth, but all of the universe.

Romans 8:19-23 "For the anxious longing of the creation waits eagerly for the revealing of the sons of God. For creation was subjected to futility, not of its own will, but because of Him who subjected it, in hope. That the creation itself will also be set free from its slavery to corruption into the freedom of the glory of the children of God. For we know that the whole creation groans and suffers the pains of childbirth together until now.

WILL THERE BE ANIMALS IN THE NEW EARTH?

Some may disagree, but I think the scripture clearly states, yes, there will be animals in heaven.

Isaiah 11:6-9 "In that day the wolf and the lamb will live together; the leopard will lie down with the baby goat. The calf and the yearling will be safe with the lion, and a little child shall lead them all. The cow will graze near the bear. The cub and the calf will lie down together. The lion will eat hay like a cow. The baby will play safely near the hole of a cobra. Yes, a little child will put its hand in a nest of deadly snakes without harm. Nothing will hurt or destroy in all My holy mountain, for as the waters fill the sea, so the earth will be filled with people who know the Lord."

WILL OUR PETS WHO HAVE DIED BE IN HEAVEN?

We don't really know. We do know God can and will reconstitute all the cells of humans and make them into a new body like Jesus (Philippians 3:20), so He could do the same for our deceased pets. Please note, there is no Biblical statement that I am aware of which speaks directly to this question.

WHAT SHOULD CHRISTIANS DO IN THE MEANTIME? (ROMANS 8:23-25)

Perhaps the wisest thing we can do is to wait patiently. It will happen!

Romans 8:23-25 "And we believers also groan, even though we have the Holy Spirit within us as a foretaste of future glory, for we long for our bodies to be released from sin and suffering. We too, wait with eager hope for the day when God will give us our full rights as His adopted children, including the new bodies He has promised us. We were given this hope when we were saved. (If we already have something, we don't need to hope for it. But if we look forward to something we don't yet have, we must wait patiently and confidently.)

WE ARE NOW GOING TO TURN TO A RATHER COMPLICATED PROPHECY FROM ISAIAH. AS HAPPENS SOMETIMES IN SCRIPTURE, SOME PROPHECY IS FOR NOW, SOME IS FOR THE FUTURE, AND SOME IS FOR THE DISTANT FUTURE. I INVITE YOU TO LOOK CAREFULLY AT ISAIAH 65: 17-25. LET'S SEE IF WE CAN DISCERN TOGETHER WHAT PARTS ARE FOR THE MILLENNIUM? WHAT PARTS ARE FOR THE NEW EARTH?

Please note, in at least 1,007 years (millennium plus seven tribulation years), the New Heaven, Earth, and Jerusalem will be made. In the meantime, Jesus will personally reign from Jerusalem over the entire earth. At the end of the 1,000 years, Satan will make his final attack on God. There is no battle, Jesus simply sends him and all of his followers to an eternal hell.

Isaiah 65: 17-25 "Look I am creating new heavens and a new earth, and no one will even think about the old ones anymore. Be glad; rejoice forever in my creation! And look! I will create Jerusalem as a place of happiness. Her people will be a source of joy. I will rejoice over Jerusalem and delight in my people. And the sound of weeping and drying will be heard in it no more. No longer will babies die when only a few days old. No longer will adults die before they have lived a full life. No longer will people be considered old at a hundred. Only the cursed will die that young. In that day people will live in the houses they build and eat the fruit of their own vineyards. Unlike the past, invaders will not take their houses and confiscate their vineyards. For my people will live as long as trees, and my chosen ones will have time to enjoy their hard-won gains. They will not work in vain, and their children will not be doomed to misfortune. For they are people blessed by the Lord, and their children, too, will be blessed. I will answer before they even call to me. While they are still talking about their needs, I will go ahead and answer their prayers. The wolf and the lamb will feed together. The lion will eat hay like a cow. But the snakes will eat dust. In those days no one will be hurt or destroyed on My holy mountain. I, the Lord, have spoken!"

WILL WE EAT IN HEAVEN?

I sure hope so. As near as I can discern there will be "vegetarians!" Now that will be a big change in itself. (I am hoping God changes His taste buds!)

Revelation 19:7 "Let us be glad and rejoice and let us give honor to Him. For the time has come for the wedding feast of the Lamb, and His bride has prepared herself."

Revelation 22:1-2 "Then an angel showed me a river with the water of life, clear as crystal. Flowing from the throne of God and the Lamb. It flowed down the center of the Main Street. On each side of the river grew a tree of life, bearing twelve crops of fruit, with a fresh crop each month.

Revelation 22: 14-15 "Blessed are those who washed their robes. They will be permitted to enter through the gates of the city and eat the fruit from the tree of life." (NLT)

WILL WE LEARN NEW THINGS? HOW DOES IT MAKE YOU FEEL TO SOMEDAY WE WILL KNOW THINGS THAT ARE JUST A MYSTERY TO US TODAY WILL BE MADE CLEAR? (I CORINTHIANS 13:12)

This is for me a major highlight of the New Heaven and the New Earth. God Himself, teaching me new things! (Who knows, maybe I'll have an eternal "man cave!")

1 Corinthians 13:12 "Now we see things imperfectly as in a cloudy mirror, but then we will see everything with perfect clarity. All that I know now is partial and incomplete, but then I will know everything completely, just as God knows me completely.

JESUS PROMISED THAT HE IS NOW IN HEAVEN PREPARING A PLACE FOR US. NOTICE: HE SAID WHEN EVERYTHING IS READY, I WILL COME AND GET YOU.

TALK ABOUT YOUR CONSTRUCTION PROJECTS. THIS CITY IS 1500 MILES CUBED DECORATED IN UNIMAGINABLE BEAUTY. NEW HEAVEN AND NEW EARTH TO HOUSE THE NEW JERUSALEM.

(I can only speak for myself, but I can't wait.)

John 14: 1-4 "Let not your hearts be troubled, you believe in God, believe also in Me. In My Father's house are many mansions, if it were not so, I would have told you. I go to prepare a place for you, and if I go, I will come back for you, that where I am, you may be also.

Revelation 21: 10-17 "So he took me in the Spirit to a great high mountain, and he showed me the holy city, Jerusalem, descending out of heaven from God. It shown with the glory of God and sparkled like a precious stone-like jasper as clear as crystal. The city wall was broad and high, with twelve gates guarded by twelve angels. And the names of the twelve tribes of Israel were written on the gates. There were three gates on each side- east, north, south and west. The wall of the city had twelve foundation stones, and on them were written the names of the twelve apostles of the Lamb. The angel who talked to me held in his hand a gold measuring stick to measure the city, its gates and its wall. When he measured it, he found it was a square, as wide as it was long. In fact, its length and width and height were each 1,400 miles. Then he measured the walls and found them to be 216 feet thick (according to the human standard used by the angel.)"

Discovery #6
RELATIONSHIPS IN HEAVEN

In the new Earth a lot of things will change. For us, we get our resurrected body with a new name.

"For our citizenship is in heaven, from which we eagerly wait for a Savior, the Lord Jesus Christ, who will transform the body of our humble state into conformity with the body of His glory, by the exertion of the power that He has even to subject all things to Himself." (Philippians 3: 20-21)

We are still the same person who received life at our initial salvation. However, it is much improved. Take a moment and discuss what you think it will be like when we see and talk with each other and our departed loved ones. One of the best things will be communication is perfect. No masks, no hidden agendas. We are given a promise from God, who by the way, never breaks a promise. Look at I Thessalonians 4:13-14 and verse 17, "But we do not want you to be uninformed, brethren, about those who are asleep, that you may not grieve, as do the rest who have no hope. For if we believe that Jesus died and rose again, even so God will bring with Him those who have fallen asleep in Jesus," (V 17) "Then we who are alive and remain will be caught up together with them in clouds to meet the Lord in the air, and thus we shall always be with the Lord."

What truths are given here that enhance our desire to be in heaven? Might I be so bold as to say, there is no doubt about it, God has promised we will see loved ones again who now live in the intermediate heaven!

Jesus never called the Church "The Bride Of Christ" but it appears Paul did. Take a few minutes and talk about how you see this relationship. I think we can unequivocally state, we are honored guests at Jesus heavenly banquet!

Note if you will, Jesus never refers to the redeemed community as bride, but rather as wedding guests. (Read Matthew 22:2-10 and 25: 1-13.)

"The kingdom of heaven can be illustrated by the story of a king who prepared a great wedding feast for his son. When the banquet was ready, he sent his servants to notify those who were invited. But they all refused to come. So he sent other servants to tell them, 'the feast has been prepared. The bulls and fattened cattle have been killed, and everything is ready. Come to the banquet. But the guests he had invited ignored them and went their own way, one to his farm another to his business. Others seized his messengers and insulted them and killed them. The king was furious, and he sent out his army to destroy the murderers and burn their town. And he said to his servants, the wedding feast is ready, and the guests I invited aren't worthy of the honor. Now go out to the street corners and invite everyone you see. So the servants brought in everyone they could find, good and bad alike, and the banquet hall was filled with guests." (Matthew 22:2-10)

"The kingdom of Heaven can be illustrated by the story of ten bridesmaids who took their lamps and went to meet the bridegroom. Five of them were foolish, and five were wise. The five who were foolish didn't take enough olive oil for their lamps, but the other five were wise enough to take along extra oil. When the bridegroom was delayed, they all became drowsy and fell asleep. At midnight they were roused by the shout 'Look the bridegroom is coming! Come and meet him!' All the bridesmaids got up and prepared their lamps. Then the five foolish ones asked the others, 'please give us some of your oil because our lamps are going out.' But the others replied, 'we don't have enough for all of us. Go to a shop and buy some for yourselves.' But while they were gone to buy oil, the bridegroom came. Then those who were ready went with him to the marriage feast, and the door was locked. Later, when the other five bridesmaids returned, they stood outside, calling, 'Lord! Lord! Open the door for us!' But he called back, 'believe me, I don't know you!' So you, too, must keep watching! For you do not know the day or the hour of my return." (Matthew 25: 1-13)

Some believe the bride of Christ is the New Jerusalem. Others say it is the Church of Jesus Christ. This is unclear, at least to me. My suggestion is for you to check it out and decide for yourself.

"Then I saw a new heaven and a new earth, for the old earth and the old heaven had disappeared. And the sea was also gone. And I saw the holy city, the new Jerusalem, coming down from God out of heaven, like a bride beautifully dressed for her husband." (Revelation 21: 1-2)

Then one of the angels who held the seven bowls containing the seven last plagues came and said to me, 'Come with me! I will show you the bride, the wife of the lamb,' So he took me in the Spirit to a great, high mountain, and he showed me the holy city, Jerusalem, descending out of heaven from God." (Revelation 21:19)

The Spirit and the bride say, 'Come. Let anyone who hears this say, come. Let anyone who is thirsty come. Let anyone who desires drink freely from the water of life.'" (Revelation 22:17)

We will be diverse and appreciate one another as never before.

"And they sang a new song saying, 'Worthy art Thou to take the book, and to break the seals; for Thou waste slain, and did purchase for God, with Thy blood men from every tribe and tongue and people and nation."

This is Perfect diversity!
Who else is There?

"And I looked, and I heard the voice of many angels around the throne and the living creatures and the elders: and the number of them was myriads and myraids, and thousands of thousands." (Revelation 5:11)

Note, there are millions, yes billions of angels, and other living things and elders. Who knows, there may very well be a lot more that we are not told about!

Discovery #7
OUR GREATEST ADVENTURE
THE BEST IS YET TO COME!

There will be a new heaven, a new earth, new relationships and new adventures we can't even imagine. Psalm 16:11, as well as many others, gives us a glimpse of this new adventure. What stands out to David in this Psalm? What stands out for us?

Answer:
Eternal joy and pleasure of living with God!

Psalm 16:11 "You will show me the way of life, granting me the joy of your presence and the pleasures of living with you forever.

John 14: 1-3 are very familiar verses. Based on what we have looked at the past few weeks, how much more do these verses excite you?

Answer:
When I die I get to see the New Jerusalem (perhaps currently being built) in the intermediate heaven, with a place in it for me.

"Don't let your hearts be troubled. Trust in God. Trust also in Me. There is more than enough room in my Father's home. If this were not so, would I have told you that I am going to prepare a place for you? When everything is ready, I will come and get you, so that you will always be with Me where I am." (John 14: 1-3)

Read Colossians 3:1-4. Paul gives some excellent teaching on what to think about in our quiet times. What new truths have you seen when you have quietly thought about these verses?

Answer:
I am what I envision and think about. These verses really elevate my mood, especially when I get in the dumps.

"Since you have been raised to new life with Christ, set your sights on the realities of heaven, where Christ sets in the place of honor at God's righteousness hand. Think about the things of heaven, not the things of the earth. For you died to this life, and your real life is hidden with Christ in God. And when Christ, who is your life, is revealed to the whole world, you will share in all His glory." (Colossians 3: 1-4)

Every person who ever lived or is alive today has a gentle tugging in their spirits that God put in them for a purpose. What is that purpose?

Answer:
Eternity in their hearts. God wants all His creation with Him for all eternity.

"He has made everything beautiful in its time. He has also set eternity in the hearts of men; yet they cannot fathom what God has done from beginning to end." (Ecclesiastes 3: 11)

Philippians 4: 5-7 are "go to" verses for our daily lives, and they are great! Scripture can, and often does, have many applications to the same verses. In light of heaven, how do you see these verses affecting your life?

Answer:
It helps to keep life in perspective.

"Let everyone see that you are considerate in all you do. Remember, the Lord is coming soon. Don't worry about anything; instead, pray about everything. Tell God what you need and thank Him for all He had done. Then you will experience God's peace, which exceeds anything we can understand. His peace will guard your hearts and minds as you live in Christ Jesus." (Philippians 4:5-7)

We have often said we have a lot more days behind us than ahead of us. Given that, and given heaven awaits us, what should we be doing now?

Answer:
Practice intercessory prayer. Keep growing in Jesus. Love more.
This concludes Bill's study about heaven. Please note, he would remind you that he has gained much of his insight from other workers of the Word. Primary among those being Randy Alcorn, David Jeremiah, Grant Jeffery, several commentators too numerous to mention, and of course the Holy Bible.

10 HOW THOSE WHO CARE, CARE

(The following is gleaned from conversations with Bill's Family, as well as several close friends)

The process of losing someone you care deeply about can be difficult, challenging, heartbreaking, and even life changing. In the case of a parent or close family member, these conflicting emotions are magnified. After all, they have always been there throughout your life, and it's difficult to imagine a future without them.

Family mealtimes, whispered words of love and encouragement, the cool wash cloth on a forehead when sick, the hugs, the affirmations of love and appreciation are now, the things you desire the most. You find yourself becoming acquainted with an insecurity never before experienced. The things you always took for granted now seem so big. Even though they have not crossed over yet, you already miss them.

Then, like a phantom, compassion fatigue sneaks in, followed closely by feelings of guilt, and self-recrimination for even allowing these thoughts and feelings a place in the journey. You don't like these times, but they still linger, often in the background, just waiting to attack at a time when you seem most vulnerable.

You tend to grasp at any kind of health news that suggests hope, and maybe you even get a break from the stress for a time. Then, just when it seems like you can relax a bit and let your guard down, bad news comes for another visit and the process starts all over. The prevailing sentiment often seems to be feeling over-taxed and tired, yet continually wanting to stay involved, available and connected.

You realize if you are going to capture any moments, now is the time. Making sure whatever interactions you have with the one you love and are losing is special, becomes a priority. Because memories are life's greatest souvenirs, you become an avid collector.

Death is something you seldom mention, but often think about. The finality, the futility of bargaining with reality and the always present sense of separation and loss dominate much of your waking time. It is in just such times as these that the Word of God can be a soothing balm. After all who would have a better grasp on this yet to be experienced journey than one who has walked this valley called death? Note the instructions given:

"God is our refuge and strength, a very present help in trouble. Therefore we will not fear, though the earth should change, and though the mountains slip into the heart of the sea." (Psalm 46 NASB)

"Therefore we do not lose heart, but though our outer man is decaying, yet our inner man is being renewed day by day. For momentary, light affliction is producing for us an eternal weight of glory far beyond all comparison." (II Corinthians 4: 16-17.)

Most realize and experience deep within their personal being (spirit) a plan for all of God's redeemed children to eventually make this journey. Without death there could be no escaping the problems, stresses and difficulties we encounter on this side. Without the reality of this spiritual transition there would be no hope for better days, no assurance of a blessed eternity, and no opportunity to experience a life without, pain, problems, and difficulties.

The apostle Paul explains this so well in his writing to The Corinthian Church; "Now I say this brethren, that flesh and blood cannot inherit the kingdom of God; nor does the perishable inherit the imperishable. Behold, I tell you a mystery, we will not all sleep, but we will be changed. In a moment, in the twinkling of an eye, at the last trumpet; for the trumpet will sound, and the dead will be raised imperishable, and we will be changed. For this perishable must put on the imperishable, and this mortal must put on immortality." (I Corinthians 15: 50-53.)

While Paul is speaking primarily about the resurrection, he makes it clear why we must one day give up this mortal body, to receive a new spiritual body. There has been much written about what that spiritual body will be like, but quite frankly, I don't think anyone has a "for sure" lock on the answer. Bill deals with this aspect of "change of identity" in his teaching about heaven. I am very happy to wrap my mind and spirit around his expose. (You can find this in his "Heaven Outline.")

Perhaps it would be spiritually refreshing to begin to look at what we call death as actually the beginning of something new and vital! Life is not over; it is just beginning. As with any new journey, there are always questions about the route, what exhibits you will take in, and who you will meet on the way. Such it is with our heavenly journey, we don't have all the answers, but we do know it's going to be out of this world!

When asked what they wanted most for Bill's travel towards the promised land, a friend's reply was, "I just want him to die well." Everyone has their own personal idea of what their end times here on earth will be like. Pain, agony, and physical difficulties are usually not on the menu of options. While we have no real choices in the matter, we can prepare.

Being spiritually ready (sins forgiven, Jesus is Lord) will without doubt make the transition much smoother. Letting those who you cherish the most know you are "ready" is a gift to those you are leaving behind.

Bill has three sons. When asked a number of questions about their feelings and thoughts of their father's imminent transition, they each responded with an assurance of his eternal destination. No questions, no doubts, no what ifs. They "knew without equivocation, heaven was going to be his permanent residence. What a gift Bill is leaving them, as well as a legacy they can live into!

I heard someone say recently, "Reality is an undefeated champion." As I have had the privilege of sharing some precious moments with Bill, he has never wavered in his knowledge of where his eternal destiny lies. Not one time has he even intimated that he is running from his personal reality, but rather, embracing it with vigor.

I think that is the definition of "dying well," which Bill's friend was referring to. My personal prayer is that I will be able to embrace my transition from this world with as much joy and positivity! That dear friend is Bill's wonderful gift to each of us. He is not only pointing the way, but also showing us the baggage we have the opportunity to leave behind.

That is all I will write for now. I have suggested to my friend that we publish this part of his story. (I really want him to see it in print.) Yes, there is still more of the story to be told. I will finish with a final chapter after his heavenly transition. His desire was for those who would read about his personal journey to know what the "final days" were like. Right now, he is keeping a daily diary of his last steps toward the finish line. It will be my privilege to share these with you at the appropriate time. Until then, - - -

11 THE LAST CHAPTER

I am really struggling with writing this final chapter. Bill and I had spent every Thursday together for two years. The idea of writing about Bill's Cancer journey began as a project and concluded with something quite unexpected. I hope I can adequately describe how a writing project morphed into a surprising friendship.

I don't think I will ever go to our local Drive-In without thinking about my friend. Every Thursday, 2 milkshakes, no whipped cream, no cherries.

Occasionally he would add a chili cheese dog to the order. (He always stipulated, only if they were on sale) In two years I can only remember them being "on sale" once. It did not matter to me, so when Bill would ask, I would just reply, they always have things on special! He always wanted to "reimburse" me, but I told him not to try spoiling my blessing.

I have two advanced degrees in Theology. Seldom would I find someone I could "talk Theology" with that had Bill's depth and insight. We had some of the most raucous discussions on everything from heaven, angels, hell and the devil, and everything in between. I so miss those times yet treasure them beyond description.

Bill made his transition to heaven on Friday December 12th 2024. Shortly before his death I was talking to him about "how he was doing?" He just smiled at me and his eyes said, "you know" and I did! It was Eleanor Roosevelt who said, "Many people will walk into your life, but true friends will leave footprints in your heart."

Ok, enough about me. I want to take you on a brief journey through Bill's last six months of life on earth. To provide some context, we finished drafting the book in October, and the plan was to send it for printing. We agreed after Bill transitioned to heaven, I would take the book down from the website and write the "last chapter." Unfortunately, the printing company could not get a proof copy completed before Bill's passing. I so wanted him to see his words in print. Every day when I would visit in those final weeks Bill would tell people, "L.D. Is bringing a copy of the book today." I still struggle with that failure.

What you will read in just a few minutes are what we called "Bill's updates." He would try to write his thoughts and feelings in capsule form. It was important to him that you, the reader, might find some personal help from his last days. So, take a deep breath, strap in, and prepare to read the words of one who is now "living" what he believed, taught, and lived!

Update Musings, June, 2024

"I have written several thoughts about the wonders of God and what He is still teaching me. As I close in on almost 10 years since my diagnosis of stage 4 Prostate cancer, I often find myself thinking back to other days. I am sure I had this disease for quite some time before being officially told I had a disease that would eventually take my life. At the time 5 years seemed optimistic. I must add, I have learned a lot about my Heavenly Father during this time, and that has been wonderful beyond words.

Early on it was unbelievably bad. The doctor told my wife that I was in the valley of the shadow of death, and we needed a family meeting. At the time I was beyond miserable. The infusions started that week. My Intercessory prayer warriors began praying. I got better, never good, but better. After that time, I have never had a really good day, but I also never had a horrendous one either. I have to say, a good medical team and friends praying for you are a great combination.

I have also had many significant challenges. They have not all been great or even good. I have accumulated over $1,000,000 in medical bills. The good news is, as of today I don't owe any medical bills! I did have many "discussions" with the hospitals, insurance, etc. Let me tell you, that can really wear a person out.

I would suggest you really know your insurance policies, and their benefits and restrictions. If you are fortunate enough to be asked to take part in a clinical trial or study, jump at the chance! Yes, without doubt, some of the side effects can and will be uncomfortable, but if you go into it with your eyes wide open, and you are "prayed up" it really is not particularly bad.

I knew from day one I would never be healed. I cannot tell you why, but I knew it. Over the years, as the disease has slowly taken over my life I have had to face a stark reality. This was a major issue for me, but one I had to come face to face with. I had to swallow my pride and ask for help. I am doing better at asking but still have not arrived.

There are other negative things I had to deal with. I was offered an "end of life" drug. I am presently taking it but wish now I had not agreed to be a part of the study. I am having more bad days, but I still say I am ok, but I tell my close friends the truth.

One more item for now, and then I will quit. Sharon, my wife of 56 years died after years of chronic pain. I have lived alone ever since. I do all the normal stuff- fix food, do the laundry, clean house, etc. But what I do have is a life of deep loneliness. I know in time my Father will call me home, but I must admit, some days it is a real struggle.

Once again, those of you reading this, keep The Father, The Lord Jesus Christ, and The Holy Spirit close, and you WILL get through it.

Update, July, 2024

I have now chosen to go into "in home" hospice care." The first phase consisted of setting me up with a case manager, a primary care doctor, Physical Therapy, Occupational Therapy, and a Hospice RN. His name is Clayton, and he is really something. Very Impressive!
Clayton and I discussed what I should be aware of moving forward. He suggested a few valuable information sites, with the caution, they were for information only.
I asked Clay point blank if he thinks I will make it to Easter. His response was a cautionary "probably not."
He did make me aware of an especially important reaction I had when I attended a funeral of one of my close friends. I felt an overwhelming sense of unexplainable sadness. My focus suddenly became, I want to have this journey to end! Relax, I am NOT thinking about taking my own life, I am just incredibly tired!

Update, August 2024

Large increased fatigue, so great I do not find the words to describe it. Added to this is a decrease in appetite. Home health will start providing vacuuming and light dusting next week. (That did not work out very well) I did not invite them back. Not their fault, just me being particular about the house. Another significant observation is an increased sensitivity to the presence of the Lord Jesus, and the Trinity. Clay ordered me a new walker. The doctor said it was ok to increase my meds 50%. I may soon need to go to doubling them.

Update September 2024

I am starting to be a little concerned about my ability to drive. Clay advised with this type of Cancer, fatigue and pain are the biggest issues. Both can and will be managed. I have good days/hours and bad days/hours.
I had a good prayer time last night and this morning.
Bad Day. I went to the bank to make a deposit. Then stopped to get gas. Almost had to call my son Jon, to pump the gas. The pain level shot up to a strong 7! I had planned to wash the car. Not today! Is it time to turn in my car keys?

Update, October 2024

Today was uneventful. Fatigue about the same. Pain levels up a little to a high 6 or low 7. Then later back to a high 5 or low 6.
I find myself starting to fade earlier than usual. The pain level is climbing back to a high 6 or low 7. I will discuss prescription delivery with Clay.

Update, November 2024

I have noticed my over all quality of life is slowing down. I find this in my demeanor, gait, and significant other areas.
I wonder what Sharon is doing now?
For some reason it seems like evil forces are trying to put me on a guilt trip. Jesus is more than their match.

Update, early December 2024

My balance is getting worse. I must say, there is still an unexplainable peace from Jesus! When getting ready for bed (2:15 a/m) I got this mental flash. It was not scripture, but rather Jesus with a beaming happy smile and waving at me and saying, "Come On."

That was the last update I got from Bill. When I would visit him, he would remind me that he had some he wanted to send yet. He never did.

My last visit with my friend was on Thursday December 20th, 2024. I brought two milkshakes, no whipped cream, no cherries. He was "in and out of sleep" as I visited with him. I really don't know if he knew I was there. There was one moment when he opened his eyes, and we shared eye contact for a few seconds. He even had a wisp of a smile when he opened his eyes. I cannot say for sure, but I think he was looking at his new home. I lost a friend and heaven gained a theologian. Enjoy everything you ever taught good friend, I look forward to seeing you again!

Crossing The Finish Line

www.ingramcontent.com/pod-product-compliance
Lightning Source LLC
Chambersburg PA
CBHW060839050426
42453CB00008B/748